Canadians

a narration of events

Suite 300 - 990 Fort St
Victoria, BC, Canada, V8V 3K2
www.friesenpress.com

ISBN
978-1-4602-5990-0 (Hardcover)
978-1-4602-5014-3 (Paperback)
978-1-4602-5015-0 (eBook)

1. History, Canada, General

Distributed to the trade by The Ingram Book Company

Dedication

A large thank you to my family,
all of whom were patient and supportive through
the seventeen years it took to knit this book together;
particularly, my partner Kate
who has a strong influence
on everything I do.

Preface

All of the events are true.

Table of Contents

There are fifty-six colour illustrations in the book.
They offer a visual taste of the place where each story occurs.
There is more information on the illustrations on page 207.

Enos Collins & Joseph Barss

The Congress of the United States
declared war on Great Britain,
June 18, 1812

Enos Collins had been a first mate on the *Charles Mary Wentworth*. He had saved his money, invested well and now he stood on the dock in Halifax, a well-attired ship owner and trader. Enos was here to buy a ship. If anyone took any notice of his interest in the fifty-three foot *Baltimore Clipper*, they might have wondered what was going through his mind. The little clipper, named the *Black Joke* had an awkward stance - two backward leaning masts, an overly long nose and full schooner rigging. She didn't look like the kind of ship a trader would be interested in. She was awkward at anchor but as many American ships travelling the North American Coast were about to find out, she was built for the speed and agility of a privateer.

Two weeks before on June 18, 1812, the Congress of the United States had declared war on Great Britain. No one in Canada knew there was a war on, until three American warships jumped the *H.M.S. Belvidera*. The *Belvidera*, a sixty-four gun cruiser, escaped the attack and nine days later entered Halifax harbour carrying news of the new war.

The coast of Nova Scotia was suddenly in the thick of it and Enos Collins had just bought the perfect ship to engage in privateering. Enos strengthened the decks, armed her with the tools of war that included one twelve-pound cannon and four six-pound cannons. The ugly duckling was now a sharp spike in the path of any enemy's road to success.

Privateering, at a time like this, was legal; a sailor could steal by any means at his disposal from any ship belonging to the country with whom he was at war. This dangerous occupation was practiced by both sides. Experienced captains were in great demand. It was important to hire a captain who could make instant assessments of the strengths and weaknesses of an approaching enemy and compare the enemy's qualities to his own ship's abilities. Such assessments were invalid unless they were adjusted by the wind, weather, place and time of day.

A privateer had to have a licence called a Letter of Marque."

Enos applied for his Letter of Marque, hired Captain Joseph Barss and waited.

Privateering was advantageous to all participants. Each ship captured was sold at auction. The cargo and proceeds of the sale were divided among the captain, crew and owner. There were one hundred and fifty American privateers wandering around off the Nova Scotia coast. To make a lot of money in a short period of time, privateers had to be intelligent and fast. Doctors, lawyers, children and the occasional clergyman signed on to get rich quick.

There was a distinct advantage for countries at war to have roving privateers. The privateers made it necessary for both sides to divide their navies into squadrons to protect the many merchant ships needed to keep a country going. The activities of the privateer reduced the number of ships available for naval battles.

When a ship was captured, the captain was forced to reduce his crew by the number of men it took to sail the new "prize" home. Gradually, the number of men available to sail and work the privateer became so few, the captains had to slip back to harbour to pick up more men to sail their ships.

On August 30 1812, the *Black Joke* sailed south along the American coast and in a short time, she became the best privateer on the east coast. Her low, dark shape made it easy to hide, sails down, black body up against the shore. She could wait unseen until an enemy ship came along, then suddenly pounce on her victim. The same trick was also a handy way to hide when stronger opposition appeared over the horizon.

Enos Collins was a happy man - captured ship after ship was sent back to him to sell or refit as another privateer. The successes of the *Black Joke* were so frequent, the sailing community in Nova Scotia began to recognize the unusual skill of Joseph Barss.

Before Captain Barss was done, his record became one of the best of privateering captains. Barss and the small ship he manoeuvred so well were so successful in reducing American shipping around the port of Boston, the Boston newspapers screamed for his capture and called for their navy to deal with the *Black Joke.*

Eventually, Captain Joseph Barss was cornered by a larger and better armed ship of the American Navy. He had too few crewmembers left to put up a good fight so rather than wreck the ship in an impossible conflict, he pulled down his flag and surrendered.

In this polite war, if a prisoner promised not to participate as a privateer any longer, he could be released. If he broke his guarantee and was caught, he was shot. Joseph promised not to participate in the war any longer and honoured his promise by taking a job as master of a schooner trading in the West Indies.

The trading schooner was the same but reassigned schooner that had captured the *Black Joke*!

The *Black Joke*, now in American hands was renamed *Young Teaser's Ghost* and was sent out to act as an American privateer. It was soon obvious the *Black Joke's* successes were due to the skills of the captain because she sailed twice under two names and did not capture a single prize. A British warship trapped her off the Nova Scotia coast and she was returned promptly to her home port of Halifax. Enos Collins bought her for a second time and sent her off under a New Brunswicker named Calib Seely. In eleven months, Captain Seely captured fourteen ships. He then felt he was rich enough and retired. This man who knew when to quit, moved to Liverpool, Nova Scotia and opened a successful business as a trader and merchant mariner.

The *Black Joke* carried three Canadian captains who captured one hundred and thirty American ships. The man who began it all, Enos Collins, used his wealth to found an early Canadian bank called the Halifax Banking Company. The Halifax Banking Company eventually became the Imperial Bank of Canada.

By 1814, the activities of Canadian privateers and British warships removed all American shipping from the east coast of North America.

A ship of the line, similar to the *H.M.S. Belvedera.*

The Black Joke

Stephen Lablonsky

Mr. Lablonsky was hiking on the west coast
of Vancouver Island. When he was approaching
the northern end of the island, he tripped and fell against
a dead tree. The tree fell, hit a large granite boulder scraping
the moss from its surface.

Carved deeply into the granite was a perfect square holding a
perfect circle with a perfect equilateral triangle inside the circle.
Twelve inches to the right, an upside down crucifix
was carved with equal precision.

Identical markings have been found
in two other places in the world.

Harry Morren

Harry Morren joined the North West Mounted Police knowing he would do well as a mounted policeman because he grew up on an Ontario farm and knew how to handle both work horses and riding horses well. Harry loved horses.

The N.W.M.P. was a cavalry unit and organized as Canada's third military organization after the army and navy. Today, since the inclusion of an air force, it is Canada's fourth military unit. The mode of transportation for the N.W.M.P. was horses so Canada adopted the British Cavalry system and added a few North American subtleties to their system. On his first day of police training, Harry was introduced to the *cavalry's way* to ride a horse.

Cavalry units had drills that demanded specific riding skills. A recruit had to learn how to wield his sword without cutting off his horse's ears and how to use a slender lance without impaling the horse and rider ahead.

Recruits learned to care for a military horse; how to break in a 'raw' horse and how to turn a horse into a useful and dependable mount. Harry paid close attention and learned his lessons well and on April 10, 1911 at age 21, he graduated and was posted to a tiny town in southern Saskatchewan.

Towns in southern Saskatchewan consisted of a few box-like structures randomly placed on a seemingly endless and unvaried flat surface. Each box had a water pump in front and a much smaller box-like structure behind.

Muddy roads separated the structures. If the town had dreams of becoming important, wooden sidewalks were built in front of the buildings. Nothing much happened as a rule but the surrounding settlers looked to these embryo towns for supplies, workers and help if things went wrong. A full time policeman wasn't needed because the townsfolk were in the habit of fixing things themselves.

A policeman in a one-man detachment might cover five or six towns and the space in between. Citizens saw themselves as a policeman's assistant and when things went wrong, they helped out. It was a good way and a fortunate situation because there weren't enough police to go around and in this fashion, more of the immense spaces that had to be policed were covered.

Harry loved his work and his horses. When a directive came down to all the one-man detachments that all Police constables were to be found only on horseback amongst the settlers and not sitting in their detachments.

Harry was thrilled. That's what he did anyway. He was a marvelous policeman, the best kind. If he heard there was a barn-raising at Kolinski's place, he was off to help; he took off his red jacket and worked with the best of them. He helped the Wallace family build corrals, then went up the road and sat with the ladies as they talked and made quilts. He'd check Bob in the corner store, use the washstand to clean up, then take tea with Mrs. Norman.

The recruit learned to care for a horse; how to break in a 'raw' horse and how to turn a horse into a useful and dependable mount. Harry paid close attention and learned his lessons well and on April 10 1911, at age 21, he graduated and was posted to a small town in Saskatchewan.

He knew everything there was to know about his region. The settlers told him their loves, hates and suspicions, fed him and let him sleep by the stove. He worked hard for his sixty cents a day. Harry was bent over pounding nails on a ranch in the south-east corner of the province, when a man rode up to tell him there was a body in Watrous.

Did he want to take a look?

She thought he was deadly handsome and he knew she was the best collector of news around.

Harry's normal demeanor was open and pleasant; he didn't talk too much so people talked to him. His bright splash of uniform was welcome at weddings, brandings and baptisms.

He knew everything there was to know about his region. The settlers told him their loves, hates and suspicions. They fed him and let him sleep by the stove. Harry worked hard for his sixty cents a day. He was pounding nails for a new ranch well away from the detachment, when a man rode up to tell him there was a body in Watrous. Did he want to take a look?

As Harry shared a meal with the Crow family, Mr. Crow told him about his suspicion that someone who didn't want to be seen, was hiding out at the Stokes' farm.

Someone else told him Charles Winfield, aka "The Bad Man of the Dirt Hills" was making a run for it. Harry followed the information and tracked Mr. Winfield through the snow for several days before he caught sight of him. His quarry spotted Harry, raised his revolver and air-conditioned Harry's stetson, then bounced a bullet or two off everything but Harry. Harry was a better shot than Mr. Winfield; he'd been taught that revolvers were a very approximate tool. To hit anything smaller than a house you had to shoot, "At the center of the mass." One shot from Harry and the culprit was on his back with his revolver in the snow.

The citizens of Roche Percee sent a man to get Harry to help them resolve their suspicions about a local hotel fire. Later, he was called out to Bromhead to find out why Leehan had shot George Sidler. At Bienfait, a settler and his son didn't want to play by the established rules. They didn't have a gun and constables were not allowed to draw a gun unless someone shot at them. Harry had to settle that argument with a pitchfork because a pitchfork was the settler's weapon of choice.

World War I broke out and Harry was introduced to a very unique problem. Many of the settlers in his area were of German origin and some of the men wanted to return to Germany to fight. The Canadian Government frowned on this because these men would be fighting against Canada. Harry's job was to stop them from escaping to the neutral U.S. This set the stage for Canada's first car chase.

When Harry got the word, once again from a settler, he put his horse in the barn and rushed across town to borrow the butcher's car. The German underground had a spy named Jake Lemm and Jake was going to sneak some men across the border.

Harry raced off in pursuit. Arresting someone under these circumstances was difficult. At the American border, there were two poles, thirty feet apart. If a person was arrested before the first pole, the driver of the car could claim he was just out for a drive and didn't intend to go all the way into the States. An arrest could not be made after the second pole because the person was in the United States.

The only place an arrest could be made was in the thirty feet between the two poles. Harry timed it perfectly. Two embarrassed men climbed out from under a blanket in Jake Lemm's car and gave themselves up.

Through the course of the war, Harry kept two hundred and ninety-eight men from joining the Kaiser's army.

Allan Fleming

To help build a system for the transportation of goods in a huge country, the Government of Canada took over Canadian Northern Railway when it failed in September 1918. As other railways ran into trouble, they were bought up and added to the government's collection. The Intercolonial Railways of Canada, National Transcontinental Railway and the Prince Edward Island Railway were added shortly after Canadian Northern. In December 1918, the Government joined them all together and named them Canadian National Railways. More railways were purchased and connected to a trans-portation system that went from the east coast of Canada to the west coast and on a branch that bent southward from Winnipeg, went all the way to the Gulf of Mexico.

The Canadian National Railway often struggled with the fact that it was built from a bunch of failed railways with little lines that ran to places seldom large enough to support the costs of the line. Another obstruction to financial success was that the railway was run by politicians who often made decisions based on political need rather than the financial interests of the railway. By 1960, the name Canadian National Railway had been abbreviated to Canadian National or "CN". Unfortunately, the logo on the engines and cars each had the three words - Canadian National Railway - and the new CN consisted of just two words abbreviated to two letters and It became necessary to undress the old cars and clothe them anew in something that was eye-catching and would tell the world that CN was a modern and progressive company.

A group within CN was given a budget and the task of finding a competent company for the design of new logos. After many presentations from competing design companies, CN settled on Lippincot and Margalese of New York. L&M, who had an excellent reputation, used their best designers on the project and in a few months made a presentation of their efforts to CN management in Montreal. The presentation was turned down.

Six months later, L&M made their second presentation that also failed and six months later a third presentation was again unsuccessful. L&M management decided to look for fresh designers and in the process of hunting around, they discovered a Canadian typographer-designer named Allan Fleming. Mr. Fleming was invited to the Lippincot & Margolese head office in New York for a meeting that would outline the needs of the project. Allan knew of the trouble L&M had in satisfying CN management and was puzzled because he had high respect for the L&M designers. On the flight from Toronto to New York, Allan settled back in his seat, closed his eyes and wondered what the breadth of the problems could be that kept L&M from success. In a few minutes his eyes opened.

He flipped over the doily that was under his glass and stared at the empty circle of white. He took out a pen and scribbled a rough rendering. Then, in careful and precise lines, he drew what is today considered one of the best corporate logos in the world.

Allan knew that he was ahead of himself. He had yet to hear all of the project requirements. He understood that if some hot-shot Canadian ambled into an office in New York and told the proud designers that he had solved their problem in an hour, they would not accept his idea. He also knew his earnings for a one hour deliberation would be small. He folded the doily in half, put it in his pocket and did not mention his solution in the first meeting.

Back in Toronto, armed with the full range of L&M's requirements, he tested his idea against L&M's needs and found it held. Over three months, he and a team of assistants produced models of rail cars of all sizes, engines, buildings, letterheads and anything else that would be expected to carry the logo.
On his return to New York, his idea was quickly accepted. He was very well paid for his idea and applauded with enthusiasm. The logo and its applications were shown shortly afterward to the executives of CN and were approved without reservation.

Canadian National Railways is Canada's largest and only international transportation system.

The transportation system includes many large ships that travel the world's oceans.

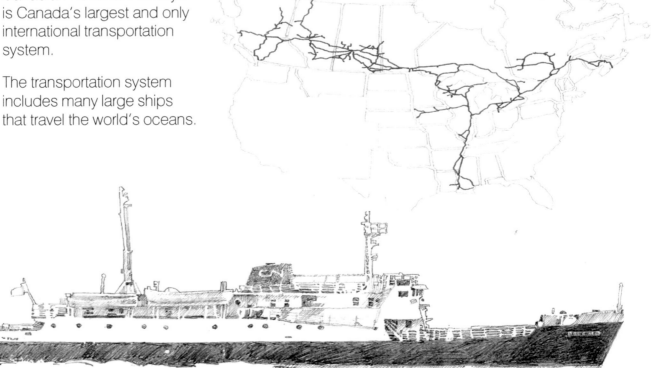

Myra Bennett

The sun turned its face under a purple skiff of cloud that edged the ruler-line horizon. The blush of warmth went away, silence cemented nightfall. Shadows faded on the simple shapes of homes. They stood holding hands leaning back it seemed from the ice-rimmed ocean. Gradually, lights came on in some of the homes. A woman cracked a door and called for an errant child.

The people at the window of the dark green house pulled their collars up, slid their hands up their sleeves and hunched against the cold. They looked like a group of turtles watching television. Of course there wasn't any television in the early years.

Inside the house Myra Bennett cleaned the kitchen table, laid out a white cloth and brought up the side board spread with tools. Myra's husband Angus boiled water and stood to assist his wife. The turtle with the best view reported the main events of the careful repair of their friend, a man who had torn his arm on a dock spike. All went well.

Myra wasn't a doctor, the only doctor lived at Woody Point. Myra was a nurse from England who had assisted the wounded in the Great War.

She read of the great need for nurses in Canada and had come over with the intention of going to Saskatchewan.

She was however, captured by the needs on the west coast of Newfoundland and settled there.

As the cleanup began, the turtles turned at a rattle of chain and harness to see a man in a logging sled riding hell-bent-for-leather towards the house. Two turtles stepped forward to catch the bridles, one entered the house to warn the Bennett's of the man's arrival and the remaining turtle gave instructions. A few minutes later, Myra came racing out of the house with her mitts in her teeth and one arm in her winter coat. The man who brought the sled put a doctor's bag by the board seat then turned the sled around. Angus Bennett, railroad lantern in hand, caught the back post and swung himself aboard.

The sled thumped and banged along a rough track that pretended it was a road, then entered a thick wood. Angus stood behind the driver, legs set for the rough ride, lantern raised to illuminate the narrow trail. Eventually, a light bloomed in the darkness and they turned down the lumber camp road to where the accident had taken place. The victim was covered in blankets, one leg twisted below the other, one ankle sawn almost through. The men had not wanted to move the leg for fear they would tear the remaining skin. Myra packed the wound first, then slowly extricated the leg with it's dangling foot. Now that the leg was out, the foot was placed in its proper position against the ankle and bound tightly. They returned to the Bennett kitchen table at a gentler pace, where the men assisted Myra in cleaning the wound and stitching up the tendons and vessels.

About two in the morning, the wounded lumberjack had his foot back on. Myra stood looking at the wound; she finally heaved a big sigh and said, "A doctor has to check this. I think it's right but we need to be certain." The next morning they packed the lumberjack into a lighter sled and stuffed him around with pillows and blankets. The west coast didn't have a road. Coastal steamers were the only way up and down but the ice had put them in drydock for the winter.

Myra, Angus and Kit the horse took the lumberjack out onto the ice and started south towards Woody Point.

The prevailing northwest wind tugged, pushed and sought out each crack in their clothing, but they kept going. They swung inland if the ice looked thin and swung out to avoid open spots where warm rivulets opened the ice close to shore. They worked along at a steady pace. About noon of the first day, they saw people coming out to check on them. One of the women in Daniel's Harbour had used the telegraph to warn the tiny communities along the coast. Women provided soup and sustenance. Men unhitched the sled to pull it themselves and give Kit a rest. Towards nightfall, someone from another community came out to take them in to a warm home. Another group provided food and accommodation for a night's rest. The trip continued in this way past Portland Creek, Parson's Pond, Cow Head, and Sally's Cove.

A woman in Parson's Pond took over the telegraph job and she busily set the aid agenda for the next day. For three days they persisted, with Angus walking at the horse's head and Myra walking beside her patient, until they arrived at Bonne Bay. As night came on, they crossed near Norris and delivered their patient to the doctor at Woody Point. The next day the doctor examined the lumberjack's foot and declared, "It is certainly as good as I could have done. If you will stay and give me a hand, we'll keep him for a while and watch his progress. Three weeks went by before they were back on the ice for the return three-day walk back to Daniel's Harbour.

Kit seemed to know where to go.

Myra and Angus Bennett had settled at Daniel's Harbour where they worked hard and hellped many. They had seven children, three of their own, four adopted.

Myra helped the sick and sewed together those who came apart. When Myra finally said she was going to retire, her family added up the years and the babies and found that she had been midwife at the birth of over five thousand babies; one of those babies was her own grandson.

Finding it impossible to turn down people in need, she pulled a tooth for a man who was eighty-six when she was ninety-two.

They crossed Bonne Bay
just past Norris Point.

Newfoundland is a part of Canada unlike any other part.

Norwegians settled the northern coast three hundred years before Columbus visited the mainland.

There is a family in Newfoundland with purple eyes.

Locals joke that all the trees
in Newfoundland
lean away from the sea.

Newfoundland fishermen are architects.

St. John's, Newfoundland's capital, surrounds a tidy harbour in the south shore of the island. An iceberg of considerable size blocked the entrance to the harbour and sat for a day, seemingly stuck, banging it's bottom on the ocean floor. A crack appeared and a chunk broke away and crashed into the ocean. When the waves settled and the iceberg had regained its balance, everyone was startled to see a Second World War bomber frozen into the newly revealed wall of ice. The following day the iceberg broke again and the bomber rolled away, never to be seen again. A man had however, taken his boat close enough to record the numbers on the aircraft. When they were checked, it was learned that the aircraft had crashed in Greenland during the war and all aboard had been rescued.

Many who visit Newfoundland express their hesitation to leave.

Matthew

Matthew was a bailiff for four Ontario counties. He was a very large and imposing man but had learned gentle persuasion worked better than physical for everyone.

His grandmother was ninety-nine and living in a nursing home. She had been a good lady who had taken time to show she cared about him. Now, he sought to give her some attention as her health declined. On a recent visit, the aging lady expressed some frustration about two situations, an unpleasant man who pestered

her and the unfortunate, bugle-like snoring of her roommate. Matthew thought about this for a while, and on his next visit, he introduced himself to the unpleasant man. They went for a leisurely walk and had a quiet and gentle talk. The pest seemed to understand the slope of the conversation and never bothered grandma again. Before leaving the nursing home, Matthew returned to his grandmother's room and gave her a water pistol. In answer to her questioning look, he explained, "It's a cure for snoring."

In 1932, there was not yet a textbook on how to fly planes in Canada's north. Each of the young pilots who flew out of Edmonton into winter temperatures as low as minus 70 degrees learned as he went.

Grant McConachie

When he finally got the goggles off with the hand that worked, twenty-three year old Grant McConachie was pleased to find he was not blind. The thing in his lap turned out to be his foot - the sole of which faced upwards. His legs were broken in seventeen places along with both hips, a few fingers and some ribs. A piece of aircraft tubing stuck through his arm pinning him to the seat.

The lesson Grant McConachie had just learned was about propeller ice.

His uncle had seen Grant's aircraft ready for takeoff and had walked across the field for a chat with Grant. The chat, while the propeller swished around in the cold air, allowed time for a fine hard ice to change the shape of the propeller. On takeoff, the plane climbed into the air without enthusiasm, limped over two trees at the end of the field and slowly lowered itself into the ground. The touch of a wingtip precipitated a cartwheel. After the left wingtip hit, the nose hit, then the right wingtip, then the tail and on and on until the thing that finally stopped was a tightly tangled ball. In the centre of the ball, Grant McConachie lay impaled, trying to figure how much of himself was retrievable.

Young Grant McConachie had not been a successful student. It took him a couple of tries at high school because his active and inventive mind was bored. He played hooky often and was caught when he wrote his own note claiming for the second time he had been at his grandfather's funeral. In disgrace at home, he ran away, only to learn that filling your stomach was more difficult than the boredom of school. He tried university but fell in love with an airplane in his second year. From that point on, Grant was not hitting the books but hitting the throttle for his "Spin of Death" at the local air show.

An exploding stove blinded two brothers named Sens. They stood without noses or faces in a cabin 150 miles north of Edmonton in a trackless wilderness. When the call went out for help, it was a very young Grant McConachie who turned up. He'd "give it a try," he said. At dawn he rose into the air with a doctor's 'how to' note and a bag full of medications. Near Pelican Rapids, he eased the plane down to spot the cabin and after two passes decided the bulrush swamp was his best bet. What came next, in bush pilot language was an "organized crash." The undercarriage bent and the fabric of the plane split from nose to tail. The plane swished out of the swamp and up to the cabin door. His singular efforts saved the Sens brothers.

One day a friend looked up as Grant flew over. He took off, running as fast as he could for the lake where he knew Grant would land. What he had seen was a bush plane with only one ski - a certain crash. He arrived at the lake where a circling Grant had found a strip of lake with bare ice next to a run of snow. Landing with one ski on snow and a broken pipe on ice was a bit rough but Grant had pulled it off again.

Grant McConachie was the first pilot to carry a paying passenger from Calgary to Vancouver. His plan was to follow the *iron compass* but when he turned left, to follow the rails west of Banff, he entered an unforgiving wall of cloud that gave not a single glimpse of the land below. He was as blind as the Sens brothers.

He followed the compass for a time but within the hour, ice began to form on the wings. Having learned that lesson well, he executed a 180 degree turn and returned to the open valley near Banff. His pride would not allow him to return to Calgary where dignitaries and the press had seen him off. Grant snuck past Calgary and flew south, then west along the border to Grand Forks, B.C. In Grand Forks, he fueled the plane and enjoyed an improvised lunch with the mayor. From Grand Forks he flew on and up to Chilliwack, then hung a left for Vancouver. His first sight of Sea Island Airport in Vancouver was a complete surprise. There were people and vehicles everywhere and they all seemed to be happily waving at him. No one had been informed of Grant's altered and extended route to Vancouver. By their reckoning, he had long since run out of fuel and crashed in the mountains.

Grant was a smart kid who knew aircraft would shrink the world. In his quest to bring the advantages of air travel to the North and later to bring modern commercial airlines to Canada, Grant McConachie became a master salesman who sold well-conceived ideas with skill and enthusiasm. He once purchased three $10,000 airplanes for a dollar each. He got a tough old prospector named Harry Oakes, to give him the biggest plane in Canada. Bush planes did not have wheels or runways and their very limited navigational supports made flying something done mostly by the seat of the pants. Planes landed on pontoons in the summer and skis in the winter - anywhere a surface looked flat enough. If the weather was socked in, planes went lower and lower until the anxious pilot could "drag a foot in the trees." On a day like that, pilots said, "eagles walk." If the route was unexplored, the pilot took a good look at a map then followed peaks, lakes and flowing water.

Grant began forming aircraft companies almost as soon as he could fly. Uncle Harry lent him $2,500 to buy a plane. Then Grant, Uncle Harry and a Maltese princess formed Independent Airways. He got help from rich Barney Phillips when he formed United Air Transport and help from others when he formed Yukon Southern Air Transport which he ran until it was purchased by

Canadian Pacific Railways. His companies were affected by the constant vagaries of commercial markets. The Great Depression slowed the flow of business for several years. Grant's airlines came and went because bush flying was a very difficult way to make a living; not only companies came and went, so did planes. One pilot made a perfect landing on a bitterly cold winter's day, taxied across the lake and slid to a standstill. Suddenly, fast as a cat, he shot up out of his seat, slit the fiber roof and jumped out onto a wing. Cold lake-water had begun to fill his boots. What he had no way of knowing was the spot where he came to a standstill, was softened by a warm spring flowing from the bottom of the lake. On this occasion, the plane was not lost but the company had to let it sit on the bottom of the lake until spring.

Grant himself had a close call when his plane lost its float plugs and sunk by the tail. Plane, passenger, mailman and cargo were saved when a partially immersed Grant threw on full power and *helicoptered* all the way across the lake. On a lake that was too short for take-off, Grant and his mechanic built a ramp up the beach then pulled the plane onto it, tied the tail to a tree and with engine at full power cut the rope, crashed down the ramp, and shortened the pines at the end of the lake by an inch.

Flying in the north was rich in adventure. Grant was in his glory and probably at his most susceptible when Barney Phillips told him the story of Black Mike McLaren. In 1945, Black Mike had come out of the Stikine with $17,000 in gold.

Two years later he went back in with a partner and neither was ever seen again. Thomas Thomas known as Dirty Tom heard the story and lacking any real evidence went to live with aboriginal people to see if he could learn anything about Black Mike's claim. He learned enough to draw a rough map but died before he could do anything with it. The map ended up in the hands of Barney Phillips. Barney wanted Grant to fly him to the secret claim but refused to show the map until they were in the air and were well on their way. They took off after telling everyone they were going to Takla Lake. Grant flew the five hundred miles to Takla, refueled and took off again. The map he was then shown had Stikine written on it so he knew he was in for a test of his skills. The Stikine area of British Columbia is the same size as Britain, France and Spain combined. Grant followed the map past Bear Lake, up Sustut Pass, slipped between two towering mountain peaks, down a frozen Injenica River to Toboggan Creek. A few minutes past Toboggan Creek, Barney pointed down. Below them was a tiny mountain lake. Grant had some doubts about the length of the landing area but down he went anyway, clipping treetops and plopping down close to the edge of the little lake. The moment the plane touched, he realized he had once again learned something new about flying in the north. The plane didn't land on the soft alpine snow. It landed under the snow and made a spectacular rooster tail all across the lake.

Barney Phillips dissapeared.

Two prospectors and their eight malamutes were picked up for a trip from Atlin to Carcross.

On takeoff, the malamutes who had never seen a plane before, panicked, ate their restraints and raced to the washroom in the rear. From there, they squeezed through a tiny hole into the tail where neither dogs nor cargo had ever been. The prospectors responded by running back to retrieve their dogs. The plane responded to the sudden change in its load by trying to fly straight up. The only answer, suggested a screaming Grant, was to cram the prospectors into the tiny cockpit to counter the weight of the terrified dogs in the tail.

The people who used Grant's airlines were a mixed lot. A jolly group of surveyors mapping the unknown regions of the Stikine, responded to Grant's gift of a bottle of rum, by naming places they mapped after Grant's pilots. Today there is a Gil's Peak, a Mount Oakes, a Kubicek Valley and an impressive mountain pass named McConachie Pass.

The stories of Grant's exploits are endless. So often when he was about to grab a little success, something came along to take it away. His positive nature made him resilient. He never dwelt on negatives and was always able to see how things could turn out well. He had learned at some point that if you stick to the things you enjoy, some version of the success you hope for will find its way to you.

When Canadian Pacific Railways bought Yukon Southern Air Transport from Grant, the company was renamed Canadian Pacific Airlines.

They also named Grant McConachie
Canadian Pacific Airline's first president.

Lillian Ailing was unhappy.

Lillian Ailing

She had emigrated from Russia and freedom in the new world just hadn't met her expectations. New York was the cat's meow for some people, but when it meant endless work at bottom wages, Lillian ran out of patience. She left her work as a hotel maid without comment.

The following day, dressed in a simple skirt and running shoes, ten dollars in a pocket and an eighteen-inch iron bar hidden in her clothing, she headed out. Lillian was going home; she didn't have enough money to buy a ticket so her only option was to walk.

She walked until the soles of her shoes were gone. She foraged for food, bathed in ponds, drank from creeks and gratefully accepted help when people were giving. With amazing persistence, she walked until she found herself in North Dakota. People were often kind and provided her with whatever they could afford to give her. She arrived in Brandon, Manitoba with new second-hand shoes. She still had her ten dollars and the iron bar was unbent. Her body had hardened and her skin was brown. Her appearance had changed a great deal from the woman who had worked inside. On the road, it was hard to keep the way she looked acceptable. Often the wind and the dirt and the shoes that were too big, gave her a rough appearance. Her pride was strong, she did not beg.

From Brandon, Lillian headed west once more. Often she slept in the corner of a field, a barn or under a bridge. Many nights she slept on the flat of the prairie in sweet smelling grass with the rumble and flash of storms around her. She walked on through rain and wind and continued in spite of many hardships. Before long she was in Regina, then "Speedy Creek." Moose Jaw, and Medicine Hat where night flyers couldn't wear blue jeans to the dance. On to Calgary and into the mountains, past Chinaman's Leap and Rundle's craggy face. Her legs must have stung from the climb up the long hill to Yoho. She passed Storm and Cathedral Mountains and walked down into the graceful valleys of British

Columbia. There were several ways to Vancouver. Her most likely route was through the Okanagan. Perhaps she slept on the shore of the hundred-mile lake. She walked with the mighty Columbia then down the raging Fraser. Which way she went no one knows for certain. We do know she arrived in Vancouver where a considerate policeman arrested her for vagrancy (the $10.00 was gone) then put her in a warm jail to keep her safe and get her ready for spring.

Jail was south, in Vancouver, so when Lillian was released in the spring she had to hike the thousand kilometres back up north to Hazelton. Rested and refreshed, she walked at a speed of 56 kilometres a day. The police kept an eye on her and asked that when she walked over the Skeena Mountains into the Yukon, to please check into each of the telegraph cabins so they'd know she was safe. They notified the men along the line that she was coming.

Bill Blackstock answered the knock on the door and was amazed to see a tiny woman in rags at his door. He held his nose and told her he was going out and she was to come in and have a bath, then he'd feed her. When he heard her story, he was amazed then concerned.

Concerned because winter was about to arrive and she had neither the clothes nor the stamina to survive a winter with temperatures that commonly fell to minus fifty-degrees.

She checked into cabin #8 in heavy snow and was again badly diminished, in rags and almost devoured by mosquitoes. The linemen convinced her to take a few days off. While Lillian rested, they rumaged around looking for pieces of their own clothing that could be cut down to Lillian's size. They gave her two pairs of socks to wear in their oversize boots so they would fit her better. These generous men, after outfitting her in better clothing, gave her Bruno the dog and made a pack for him so he could carry her supplies.

This drawing is a copy of the only photograph ever taken of Lillian Ailing.
The photograph was taken by the men who worked to repair her wardrobe.
They have put a hood on an old shirt and used it to help the hat fit her better. She is wearing a flannel shirt and heavy pants whose legs have been cut short. It appears the men were proud of their efforts and she was brave enough to allow them the picture.

By September, she had done 225 kilometres

Her next challenge was an 8000-foot mountain pass covered in fog. Jim Christie went with her as far as the pass. On the line ahead, men were trying to make it easier for Lillian. At cabin #10, Scotty Ogilvie decided to check both the trail and the cable ride that crossed the Ningunsaw River. He died when a piece of the trail, undercut by the fast moving river, collapsed and threw him in.

Still determined, Lillian tramped on over the mountains and into the Yukon where Mr. Lokken offered to help and rowed her across the Yukon River. At Pelly Crossing, Mr. Shafer took her over the Pelly. South of Dawson, a survey party took her in during

a bad storm. When the weather cleared, they gave her a small boat to float down to Dawson. *This is a little confusing because south of Dawson, the Yukon River flows north so you have to go down river to go further north.*

Wise now to northern weather, she wintered in Dawson and took time to repair another boat. In the spring, she took her boat 1400 kilometres down river to Nome, Alaska.

North of Nome on the shores of the Bering Sea, an Eskimo gentleman saw Lillian pulling a two-wheeled cart with a stuffed dog on top. He said he had never seen a white woman before and was too frightened to speak to her.

Her best chance of a successful crossing, was one hundred miles north of Nome.

No one knows if the tiny woman who had walked 9,700 kilometres was able to cover the last 80 kilometers of her trip and cross the Bering Sea into the Union of Soviet Socialist Republics.

Mr. English

S.S. Ethie

The storm that growled out of the blackened northwest sky on November 10, 1912, was not like any storm anyone had ever seen before.

As she pulled away from the dock at Parson's Pond and turned in the bay, the *S.S. Ethie* showed her sturdy profile to the land. To those who had placed a friend or relative aboard, the sight was reassuring that all would be well on her trip to Bonne Bay. She was a four hundred and forty ton single decked, two-masted steamer with two funnels and two coal fired engines below. The captain's bridge was at the front and behind him, an extensive lounge kept the sixty passengers safe from the weather. The passengers loved the trip. It was an occasion to reacquaint themselves with the news of friends and families along the coast.

The *S.S. Ethie* was part of the Newfoundland Coastal Service. She ran from Bay of Islands to the top of Labrador, stopping at all the coastal communities in between. There weren't any roads along the coast so the coastal steamer was the only way up or down. *Ethie* had faced many a storm that had blown their worst against the West Coast of Newfoundland. She had faced the worst and thought there was nothing more to see. The storm that growled out of the blackened northwest sky on November 10, 1912 was not like any storm anyone had seen before.

The wind grew to hurricane strength and the snow swirled, Captain English gradually turned the bow of the ship into the wind until she was sailing straight away from the shore. The call for full speed came as the light failed. In the morning after a full night at full steam, they were closer to the rocky coast rather than farther away. All through the next day, Captain English kept her at full steam headed west. They got no closer to their destination and again they were forced closer to the shore. It was obvious if the storm didn't ease, the ship was going to break up on the coast. A review of their fuel supply showed them they were close to empty. The wind kept its strength; Captain English asked the men to inform the passengers to prepare for the worst.

The area of shoreline they were now skirting was well known to purser Walter Young. When consulted, he said there was no cove or corner to safely ground the ship, but there was a gravel beach at Martin's Point that might provide a softer landing than the granite teeth along the rest of the shore. Two Salvation Army women led a group in prayer. Men discussed the problem. A woman with a baby in her arms sobbed. Brine grew on everything. The Prosper brothers locked arms.

Without power and blown to shore by the wind, the ship entered the surf. Her nose dug deep as the propeller stuck up into the wind. The stern buried itself as the prow reached up to grab a breath of air.

Huge waves washed the deck and livestock that were tied down, disappeared in a blink. Ice locked the lifeboats in an unbreakable grip. On a lunge, wrapped in a huge wave, *Ethie* found a hidden boulder well out and landed on it with a horrendous crash. The portholes popped. She slid off the boulder into deeper water closer to the beach but it was still well out in the thundering surf when she went aground on an underwater boulder.

The men on the *Ethie* chopped a lifeboat out of the ice and tried to get it afloat but it was reduced to kindling in seconds. Now there was only one way to save everyone and that depended on the people who had gathered on the shore.

People who live beside a road put the face of their homes towards the road to watch the things that move along that road. For the people along the shore of western Newfoundland, the ocean was their highway and they usually chose a view that looked out onto the water. Many eyes watched the struggles of the *S.S. Ethie* that day and even though the storm had taken out the telegraph wires, there was a small crowd on the shore watching and waiting as she smashed and crashed her way to a rope's-length from the shore.

History lets us down a little bit here. Different versions of the story give us different details. One story says it was the Newfoundland dog that swam into the surf to bring the rope ashore. Another says it wasn't a Newfoundland dog; it was a small noisy mutt. Another says there was no dog at all, just a man who waded in to claim the rope and bring it to shore. We do know that when the lifeboat attempt failed, the crew of the *Ethie* tried to fire a rope to the shore but the rope didn't reach far enough.

Finally, a floatation device like a barrel floated the rope close to shore where it became tangled in rocks and heavy surf. Either a big dog or a little dog or a man went out and pulled the rope to shore and tied it to a tree. The ship's crew pulled the rope tight and rigged a boson's chair to ferry the passengers ashore.

The passengers were cared for by the people of Martin's Point. Captain English was applauded for his handling of the ship in trouble.

The first passenger ashore was a wide eyed mother with her baby riding in a post office mailbag. The other sixty passengers followed safely, then the thirty-one crew members and the captain. Finally, the crumbling ship was empty and all were ashore.

In the summer of 2002, chasing other stories and visuals, I stayed overnight in a Prince Rupert bed and breakfast. The B&B was in the harbour and had several visitors that night.

In the morning, I climbed a flight of stairs to a small kitchen to search out the promised breakfast. An attractive woman, Mrs. Gould, was already at the table and she was in the mood to talk. She and her husband Bob operated an "adventure" business on the Stikine River. In full flight in an enjoyable conversation she suddenly said "and Bob was in a friend's antique shop and he dusted off a large dog's collar." The collar held three medals one of which read "Hero, S.S. Ethie."

The collar was given to Newfoundland by generous Mrs. Gould and now resides in a museum where you can view it at your liesure.

Charles Taylor

The children on the beach remember him as very tall and thoughtful.
He seemed a skeletal heron in slow motion,
out of their reach and a little forbidden.

He spoke seldom and carefully, perhaps aware of his status as a visitor from outside the family.

Tiny Thormaney Island in Buccaneer Bay was a young person's paradise with stone walks to secret places, granite walls, delicious seclusion and a Pacific tide that brought new treasures with each advance and retreat. Kids ran and crawled and snuck and searched and lay on the hot sand.

Once a week a ship would enter the bay and rudely bellow its arrival. Small craft rushed out as a huge door slid to reveal a hole in its cliff-like side - another week of supplies to fill the larder of the twenty or so homes on the island.

Bill's best memory was that Charles was a guest at Buccaneer Bay because he was courting fair Margaret. In Bill's mother's assessment, the two downsides to Charles Taylor were that he came from Toronto and he was not as dashingly handsome as she would have liked. Bill's mom had been close to her sister's children so when this fellow came along and wanted to steal her niece, she just couldn't work up any enthusiasm for the match.

He came however, with good credentials; he was a doctor, the son of a doctor, a member of the Royal Canadian Air Force Medical Corps during the war, fourteen years of university and a member of the same spiritual community as Margaret's family.

Arms extended as wings, Bill crashed on the barnacles and ripped the skin from his shin. His mother rushed him to where the doctor was staying and asked for his opinion. Doctor Taylor was unable to produce a miracle cure. That was it for Charles Taylor.

In November 1943, Charles married delicate and graceful Margaret Oliver. They moved to Calgary, Alberta where the medical fraternity eagerly awaited the arrival of their new doctor. Calgary still had a little wild west in it, wagons crashed and men fell from horses. The burgeoning city had never before had the benefit of a real neurosurgeon.

Calgary's first repairer of heads was an endlessly interesting and useful man. Aside from the obvious benefits of a person who could repair seriously broken people, he initiated the construction of professional neurological and neurosurgical facilities that serve Southern Alberta to this day. He played an active role in the administration of both Calgary General and The Foothills Hospital.

He helped to raise five vital and attractive children, took an active part in his spiritual and workday communities, walked the high trail from Lake Louise to Lake O'Hara and helped his sons rebuild an old Model T.

In church on Sunday, it was a common occurrence to see someone tiptoe quietly to the place where Dr. Taylor sat with his family. The intruder would bend and whisper into the doctor's ear then depart. A moment later, Charles would stand and with his distinctive walk, move slowly toward the door and open and close it silently. Smiles would light the faces in the rows of lowered heads as his Hollywood muffler roared and tires squealed as he raced off to repair another damaged Albertan.

Rod Stamler

The man who sat at the beginning of the front row in the graduation picture for R.C.M.P. training in June 1957, didn't want to be a policeman. He was a flyer and had his heart set on becoming an R.C.M.P. Air Division pilot.

To the men he trained with, he appeared to be just an ordinary fellow with a quiet manner and a genuine smile. He did everything well but there was no hint in training of the heights Rod Stamler's career would take him.

All of the positions for pilots were full and knowing he had to be patient to win his turn, Mr. Stamler did his 200 miles a day on highway patrol out of Saskatoon, Saskatchewan. He chased petty thieves, looked for lost children and investigated violent deaths. The structure of the law and the way it was applied began to fire his interest. His interest in flying machines paled. He met Anne, his wife-to be in Saskatoon and to comply with R.C.M.P. marriage rules, moved to Ottawa to patrol the National Capital Parkways.

In Ottawa, he applied to the Force to support him in a law degree. The course that he completed in his spare time, took six years. Finding he was into something he was good at, he took on additional studies in the areas of tax and corporate law. The R.C.M.P. had become aware of fraudulent activities inside Canadian businesses and set up a nation-wide Commercial Crime Branch. Rod, who had made a name for himself as the kind of prosecutor who designed "bullet-proof"cases, was accepted as an investigator. From this point until his retirement, Rod Stamler built an amazing record of intricate and successful investigations.

His team's long and careful exposure of the Hamilton Harbour Fraud resulted in the executive officers of twenty-one corporations being charged with fraud. The fraud involved laundering money, distributing drugs, phony invoices, inflated quotes, kick-backs to politicians and *fixed* prices for quotes.

Dredging that was not needed was done at inflated prices, via a system that drained money from the taxpayers pockets, into the pockets of fraudulent businessmen. Mr. Stamler's exhaustive investigation put them in jail. An investigation into Buffalo Oil & Gas was so complex, it was like earning a degree on how to cheat and steal. In that case, Stamler's team tricked a con man into thinking he had been caught. The man had been using Mafia money to manipulate the price of a certain stock. His only way out he was told, was to tell all. The con man told all. The Mafia ordered him killed and the fellow was hidden in an out-of-use hanger in Gore Bay. The cover story for the man who was suddenly living in a hanger was that he was an environmental scientist. The con man played his part so well the people of Gore Bay were ready to support him in a run for mayor.

Mr. Stamler proved his value as an investigator. His work in the Sky Shop Scandal resulted in the arrest of a Senator, the President of the National Hockey League and four others for fraud against the

Government of Canada. His career continued to follow an interesting path when he was sent to the National Defense College in Kingston into a course that took him to countries on every continent to learn social, economic and security issues relevant to Canada. On his return home, he was made Director of Drug Enforcement and became the Canadian representative to the United Nations Commission on Narcotic Drugs.

When one of his investigations touched on federal politicians, he was called to the centre block of Parliament Hill and taken to the office of the Prime Minister. Nose to nose with Pierre Elliott Trudeau, a former law professor, Mr. Stamler was told, "There will be no interference with any of your investigations." Further he was assured that if a member of Trudeau's political team interfered with Stamler or was shown to be tainted, he would strip that person of his authority.

Interacting with Trudeau, Jean Chretien and Ontario Attorney General Roy McMurtry, Stamler's spirits were lifted by the character of honest men who supported the rule of law. In 1988, Mr. Stamler, as second in command of the R.C.M.P., was appointed Director of the Commercial and Economic Crime Directorate and remained in that position until his retirement in August, 1989.

Then Rod Stamler bought an airplane.

The plan was to shoot
images of tough & healthy Alberta Cowboys

Alan Sneath

Allan Sneath worked for McKim Advertising in Montreal. McKim was Canada's oldest advertising agency and had been responsible for many effective communicating concepts including Canada's first bank ads.

The film production house director received a phone call from Allan Sneath on Sunday. He requested the director be on a plane to Calgary the following day with a cameraman, a crew of filmmakers and a pair of running shoes because the commercials he had to shoot must be completed very quickly.

An explanation on the plane included the information that a person who watched the activities of American owned Marlboro Cigarettes for Canadian owned Imperial Tobacco, had warned Imperial Tobacco that Marlboro was going to introduce their cigarettes into Canada. A strong and well advertised brand name like Marlboro would do Imperial Tobacco's brands considerable damage. The 'spy' who seemed to have very specific information, claimed Marlboro's first step would be to run test commercials in Peterborough, Ontario.

Allan Sneath's job was to make three competing commercials that could run in Peterborough at the same time. The Marlboro images were of very strong, healthy looking Montana cowboys riding, roping and living in the outdoors. Allan's plan was to make commercials with images of strong, healthy, Alberta cowboys. Marlboro had the advantage of time but Imperial Tobacco had an interesting advantage of its own. Several years before, a smart Imperial executive had purchased the rights to the name Marlboro for use in Canada.

In need of a new name for their product, the Americans took their Marlboros, rewrapped them in a package showing the name Maverick. Allan Sneath's commercials for Imperial Tobacco would carry the name Marlboro with a rewrapped Imperial Tobacco cigarette.

Meanwhile, back at the Rafter Six Ranch near Canmore Alberta, the director bounced along in an old truck shooting a stampede of thirty horses and two cowboys.

With that segment completed, they raced over to the Kananaskis River to film a pack train of mountain horses, led by the same, freshly mounted cowboys. The following morning, the director and his crew arrived early at Horseshoe Canyon near Drumheller. They pulled into the viewpoint above the canyon at 3:00 a.m. to catch a sunrise that was to appear at 4:30 a.m. At 4:00 a.m. the camera, crew and cowboy were ready but the man with the single sheep that the story needed, had not arrived. At least the worried director didn't think he had. Finally in a desperate state, he went over to the only other car in the parking area and woke the man who was asleep at the wheel. "Of course I have the sheep," he said. "It's in the trunk." When the trunk was opened, a sheep that had never seen a car before, became airborne. The sheep owner fought the leaping, bouncing, frantic animal down into the canyon, found a few blades of grass, tethered it and left it in peace

The story the filmmakers were shooting was about a handsome cowboy who looked all day for a lost sheep until, as the sun set, he came upon it beside the canyon wall. The earlier searching portions had already been shot and the sunrise that was to pretend it was a sunset, was what the crew was attempting to shoot.

The sun was an inch above the horizon when the cowboy spotted the sheep and rode towards it. The sheep that had never seen a car, had also never seen a horse, so as the large dark thing with a man on it approached, the sheep pulled its stake and ran for its life. It should be mentioned that in addition to the problems the director already had, the horse had never seen a sheep. When the sheep bolted south, the horse bolted north.

The cowboy was good at his job; he rode the horse to submission, then gently led it to the patch where the sheep had been and tied it to a stone.

He turned to the harried director. "If you would bring the sheep back and give me five minutes, I will make it possible for you to finish your shot." The director, if a little doubtful, was thrilled.

The sun was a foot above the horizon. Ten minutes later, the sheep was lifted and placed in the arms of the cowboy. Asking eveyone to step back, he proceeded to walk in circles around the nervous horse. The smell of the sheep began to mix with the smells of the man and the sheep/man that was walking circles around him, became less frightening. The horse calmed and the man/sheep moved closer until the cowboy was rubbing the sheep back and forth along the horse, again mixing smells. Quietly, the cowboy said, "Roll the camera please" and hearing the camera start, he gently lifted the sheep onto the horse's withers then swung aboard behind it. The rising sun was only a little bit past where it should be for sunset.

The commercials were edited in time and sent off to the Peterborough T.V. stations.

The Canadian cigarette ads were shown on the same day in Peterborough, as the American cigarettes. Stores displayed the two packages side by side. Smokers were confused and both products were dead in a week. The Americans withdrew, their attempt to launch a cigarette into the Canadian market failed. The Marlboro name went back to bed in a vault in Montreal.

Mr. Sneath smiled a little smile.

A Tall Man and a Short Man

The two met on the train west. They were
opposites in structure, one long and clerkish in
appearance, the other square and strong. They
found many subjects to share on the long trip
and became friends.

Their favorite subject was the many benefits of their new life; their favorite complaint was the hard wooden seats. "Reminds me of a pew in church," one growled. The other agreed. "Designed to keep you awake through the sermon." They were pleased when it turned out they were headed for the same place and they were filled with antici- pation when they arrived. Moose Jaw wasn't much to look at but it had a Land Office and that was where they were headed.

Their ticket in hand for a piece of land, they made arrangements for transportation. "About a day's travel north then a day's travel east," the wagon driver explained to the taller man. "We kin drop your friend off 'bout half way 'n we kin start in the morning soon's he gets his lumber."

With promises of future visits, the two men went their separate ways. The tall man, the driver decided, missed his friend because when they turned onto the eastward track, he became quieter and was not as willing to chat. The road now became a track without ruts, prairie grass flattened by hooves and wheels.

The track detoured around two lakes with no water, white alkali powdered the center, dried reeds circled the fringe. By late afternoon as they approached the tall man's land, the trail was invisible. A moon hovered on the eastern horizon. As the sun sank below the western horizon, the earth lifted its purple shadow into the pink and green sky. The shadow met the moon. The tall man shivered.

The sun cut the horizon about four in the morning, the lumber was loaded by five, and the three men were off by six. They stopped by a creek for a small lunch, then continued north for the rest of the day. The road that had begun clearly defined and well traveled became a simple track, then two ruts with a grassy center.

They met a Jewish family who were fifty miles from where they thought they were and a policeman with a dead body in a wagon. That night the weather looked like it would hold so they camped in the open. In the morning, they took a detour to drop off the shorter man with his tools and lumber. The land he had been lucky enough to get, included a spring with good fresh water, all in a pretty valley. He was ecstatic.

At one point in the night, the wagon driver awoke to find the tall man standing, wrapped in a blanket, looking skyward. Thinking there might be some- thing interesting to look at, he let his eyes run over the black ceiling of the prairie. Nothing new. Stars were bright. The Milky Way flowed across the top, the dippers dipped and an occasional shooting star made a dash for here or there.

The light of the moon made a soft blue daylight with black shadows. On the horizon, a row of thunderheads revealed their form in reflected light, a flash here, a bloom there, an ice pick of brilliance spiked here, then there. God played drums and rolled boulders. "S'ok?" he asked and the tall man jumped, startled by the sound of the driver's voice.

In the morning, the driver found the tall man looking a little the worse for wear.
When asked how he was, the tall man turned his head and the driver
was startled to see, not illness or exhaustion, but terror in his face.
They ate a hurried breakfast in silence,
collected the hobbled horse and got
the driver ready for his return trip.
"I'll be coming back with you.
Same price?" questioned
the man, "Same price,"
agreed the driver and
was wise enough not
to ask any questions.

The tall man, the driver
and the short strong man
all met again many times.
The tall man went back to
town, sold his ticket and
bought a country store.
He lived happily there until
the end of his days. If he had
to travel, he traveled in a covered
carriage and pasted newspapers
over the windows to shut out the
terrifying sky.

The driver was rewarded for his restraint with a
lot of the delivery work a country store requires. Near
the spring of fresh water, the short, strong man built a
small cube of a home with one window and a chimney
out the top. On the day he completed his house, he
put down his pipe and climbed to the edge of the valley.
As he turned and looked down at his handiwork, the
embers from his pipe ignited a fire that burned his new
home to the ground.

With the help of new neighbours, he built his home
again. The second home was "a little better" he
laughed, "cause I've had experience at this sort of
thing."

Dearest Dorothy:

If you're wondering about Judy and Jake,
they got thoroughly married in May. The day they
moved in Dad said they're going to have a baby
in nine months and fifteen minutes.

The Dudleys are ok.

His farming experience in England stands him in good stead and he's not afraid to work. Last winter he got to missing his pub so he hitched up a team and rode thirty-five miles to town for a go at the local bar. Took his boy with him to play with the kids in town. 'Round about noon the boy started to hear about the storm that was coming. He dropped by the bar and found his father in thick conversation with two other men. The boy told his father about the rumours of a storm but his father did not seem concerned. As the sun set and the sky darkened, it began to snow. The boy and his dad were finally on their way by dark. The snow was horizontal.

An hour later, the drifts made it impossible for the horses to pull the wagon any farther. Mr. Dudley unhitched them from the wagon, took off their harness, and set one horse free.

They got up on the other and proceeded on. By that time they couldn't see past the horse's ears. Mr. Dudley had never seen a storm like it, but he had a flask to stoke his courage. He released the reigns to let the horse find his own way home. On and on they rode, blind in the blizzard. The boy hung on behind and got his warmth from both horse and father. The time when they should have reached home came and went. The wind blew from the left and the wind blew from the right; it roared and hissed and tried to blow

them off the horse. They rode and rode and rode. Just when they thought they couldn't take it any longer, the horse stopped.

Peering forward past the horse's ears, they could make out a barn door. They jumped down, opened the door, put an old blanket on the horse and snuggled into the hay. They knew it wasn't their barn but the hay would keep them warm till morning. Wakened at first light by the owner of the barn, they were queried about where they were from and what they were doing in his barn. Mr. Dudley explained what had happened and where they were from. " I thought if I let the horse go on his own he would take us home." "He did," was the surprising response. "This is where he was born. You bought him from me four years ago at the Red Deer Fair. That's his mother in the next stall."

In working out what had taken place, Mr. Dudley discovered the moment the horse was free (about five miles from their farm) the horse had done a loop back towards town, through the outskirts of town and then thirty miles out the other way to the farm where he was born. Mr. Dudley and his son learned a little more about horses that day. Each animal has a different personality all its own, just like people. Mr. Dudley is still looking for the horse he set loose in the blizzard. Nobody knows where it was born.

Haven't been able to call anyone for a while. George, your distant uncle, decided he would teach the two boys how a lumberjack cuts down a tree. He took the two up to the top of our road where a tree had lost a limb and looking like it might come down in a storm. He showed the boys how to look closely at the tree to see which way it might naturally fall; then how to decide where they wanted it to go and where to cut a notch in the side.

They went to the other side and whacked away at it with the axe until there was a notch six inches above the first notch. The deeper notch dictates the way the tree falls. George was in full flight with his explanation when a gust of wind decided to show the boys how a tree falls. The tree came down with a mighty crash, the wrong way, and it took out all the telephone lines. The lines were on those poles that have three cross bars braced below with two strap iron braces. Each cross bar has fifteen glass insulators on pegs and a phone line that can carry three calls, neatly tied to each. Add them up and that makes forty-five lines with a minimum of one hundred people talking on them.

Macy swears the Prime Minister was on one and there were a lot of important people on the others. Anyway Uncle George isn't showing his face much. The two boys have been very decent about it, not whispering or giggling when George is around. George admitted the lumberjacking was a failure and wondered if they knew he used to box. Did they want to learn how? They knew he didn't have his left eye so both graciously declined, fearing some unknown disaster. Dear George, he and Nancy don't have any kids of their own and he tries too hard to be a good uncle.

Ruby continues to work hard. She takes care of Betty's babies all day, then goes and does an evening shift in the mine. Fills boxcars with a shovel, then walks home in the dark. Had a fall of rock but it missed her.

We had the Tetleys over; he's the one who sucks his teeth. Can't finish a sentence without a ghastly sucking in of breath between clenched teeth. Gas in the War. He was telling us what happened to his son. I had always wondered. It was very emotional but I think the telling freed him up a bit. I think this all happened after you left. Anyway, his son loved to farm and the Tetleys had retired and turned over a splendid herd for him to manage. The idea was that the son's success with the herd would help to support the two of them in their old age. The big storm of '17 crawled out of the northeast. The sky went black and before the snow began, it whipped up dirt so bad you couldn't look that way.

As cattle are wont, they put their tails to the wind and let their butts take the brunt of it. They walked for four days before the wind and the cold.

Where there were fences, the cows crowded into the corner until they froze and the oncoming cows walked over them. Where there were no fences, they walked until they couldn't walk any more, then froze to death standing up. Fell down with the thaw in the spring. In a manner of speaking, Mr. Tetley's son fell down too. He's been in the institution at Panoka ever since. He should've had a woman to help him through such a terrible thing. Some say we have a hard life, maybe we do but I wouldn't trade it. The kids that live in town got their hands on some cardboard and they're roaring down the hills on the pieces for as long as they last. An expensive toboggan couldn't give a better ride in winter. They have to watch for the little cactus but the grass lets them go at an amazing clip.

Harold is drop dead handsome and the Indian who used to watch Grandma make buns doesn't come by the farm anymore.

Drumheller is growing. There's a store in town that has pretty much everything we need. If what we need isn't there, we can get it out of Calgary pretty quick.

This summer a woman and her teenaged daughter moved into town. They weren't accepted for a while but she took to teaching piano and folks got to like her. Now she's the town favourite because she and her daughter play the piano together at 7.00 o'clock every evening. All the windows in that part of town are opened and people sit by their window to listen.

Harry Walchuk's kind of gone on her. We think she should get together with old Mr. Sankey who plays his bones till two in the morning. Probably Bobby Blair will get her. He's made a fortune on pelts this year. The Cattleman's Association pays $100.00 for wolf.

$$$$$$$$$$$$$

We needed lumber for the new barn, so the boys rafted some logs down the Red Deer River. Since they had to make the trip anyway, they put the piano on the raft and brought it along too! When I play my piano, it sounds like I'm playing with my elbows. I keep my windows closed.

At Halloween, the kids were quiet, but it was only because they were working on a plan. Apparently one of their teachers does a lot of his work sitting in his outhouse. His overcharged students waited for the right moment, tipped his "office" and ran.

So now you're up to date. I'll take this over to the Armstrong place and leave it for the postman who comes around once a week. Maybe they can lend me an envelope.

Love, Betty
P.S. Chief's back, brought a gift.

Fredrick G. Creed

In 1938, Mr. Creed, an inventor from Winnipeg, presented an idea for a twin-hulled aircraft carrier to the British Admiralty. He was rebuffed. In 1941, he showed the idea to the U.S. Navy and was again turned away.

Today, seventy years later, his idea has caught on and is becoming the more common method of construction for specialized ocean-going craft.

Mr. Creed's idea was expensive but held huge benefits. The design, suggested by the fact that submarines at periscope depth are not affected by heavy seas, consisted of two submarine-like hulls side by side and submerged under the ship. In heavy seas with huge waves, the decks of large ships could be kept level and calm.

An ocean liner named the *Radisson Diamond*, now carries hundreds of passengers without the sea sickness that is common to sea cruises. The Canadian Coast Guard uses his idea to make a stable platform for observational duties. U.S. surveillance ships and a U.S. Navy Stealth ship have been built, as well as stable helicopter pads and gun platforms for the military.

In 2007, there were forty ships, and plans for the construction of many more that will use Mr. Creed's invention.

Jeremiah Albert Jones

Jeremiah Albert Jones was born in Jollytown, Upper Brookside, Colchester County, Nova Scotia.

On June 16 1916, after three tries, Mr. Jones enlisted in the 106th Battalion of Canadian Forces and headed overseas to fight in the First World War. In France, the 106th was split up to reinforce depleted regiments. Mr. Jones joined the Royal Canadian Regiment just in time for the ferocious fight on Vimy Ridge. In the midst of the worst fighting, Jeremiah single handedly captured a German machine-gun post and escorted its surviving members and their gun back to Canadian lines.

Mr. Jones was recommended by his officers for the Distinguished Service Medal but never received it. Jeremiah Albert Jones was black. Many Canadians of African heritage fought to join the Army and were told, "This is a white man's war." When conscription was implemented, the colour bar disappeared.

Emma Edmonds

Emma was born in the rural settlement of Magaguadavic, New Brunswick. Her family needed a boy more than a girl, so she laboured on the farm as a boy. When she was fifteen, her father decided she was going to marry someone she didn't like.

She left home and to escape her father's wrath, she changed her name to Frank Thompson and got a job in Moncton selling bibles. She went south and joined the Union Army as a male nurse, became a post-master, got a job as a Union spy, worked as an Irish immigrant, a black slave and a confederate trooper.

Eventually she returned to New Brunswick, married Lynus Seeleye and made a family.

Ross Hamilton

Lieutenant Ross Hamilton enlisted in the 9th Ambulance Corps in World War One, where he took part in the heavy fighting in France.

In World War Two, he was an active member of the Army Medical Corps.

Early in his military career it was discovered that he had a beautiful soprano voice. To entertain the troops in both wars, he played the part of "Marjorie" in a troupe called the Dumbelles and entertained the fighting men in both wars.

Samuel Benefield Steele

Sam Steele has been a sailor,
a bare knuckle boxer, a store clerk and was
the third man to join the North West Mounted Police.

At sixteen years of age, young Sam Steele was asked to assume the leadership of the Clarksburg Militia. He refused, claiming he was too young and had too much to learn. This wise decision was the product of his upbringing and the education he had been given by his father.

Captain Elmes Steele was a Royal Navy hero of the Napoleonic Wars who had been awarded a 1000 acre homestead in Simcoe County, Ontario.

At nineteen, Samuel joined the 1st Ontario Rifles on their march west to protect Fort Garry from the Fenian raiders. The six-hundred-mile-walk from Thunder Bay to Fort Garry was a wild mix of portages, rock, heavy bush, mosquitoes and black flies that gave him an appropriate introduction to life in the military.

When the threat to Fort Garry subsided, Sam came home and attended Kingston Military College at Fort Henry. When he finished his courses, he joined the Canadian Army. He was the twenty-third man to become a Canadian soldier.

The Prime Minister asked for the formation of a military group that could help families migrating west and protect aboriginal nations from those who would misuse them. Sam saw the need and switched from the Army to the North West Mounted Police. He was the third man to join and because of his military training, was given the rank of Sergeant Major.

The winter of 1884 found Sam back in Fort Garry with recruits he had chosen. When he had shaped them into the kind of policemen he needed, they became the first men to bring the rule of law to the west.

Sam taught his men to follow the foundation his father had given him - treat all people fairly, politely and maintain the rule of law. The men who did not understand the concept of respectful policing, went away. The wiser men stayed and learned that policemen make better decisions when they learn the ways, the language and the beliefs of the people they police.

To help his men understand the aboriginal people, he told them a story he cherished. An aboriginal man had gone to great lengths to find Sam to give him a cookie. The man explained he had been very hungry and had taken a cookie from a police cache. Now that he had found Sam, he could replace it.

"If aboriginal men are honest, why do they steal horses?" a recruit asked. Sam explained that taking horses was an established and historic, socially acceptable custom young aboriginal men used to prove their courage. In their culture, stealing horses was more a risk-filled game than stealing.

As soon as men and horses had recovered, regular patrols were instituted out of Fort Edmonton. Policemen learned the ways of new aboriginal groups and did their best to treat both aboriginals and whites with fairness and respect.

Sam received an increase in rank.

Sam's cookie story was a reminder for his men that when they were dealing with the aboriginal people, they were dealing with a legitimate culture.

In the United States, mayhem reigned. The fighting never stopped because respect and permanent rights were denied the aboriginal people. The aboriginal people called the boundary between Canada and the U.S., the *Medicine Line*. The Red Coats above the line were good medicine and the American soldiers below the line were bad medicine.

Roche Percee

Now trained and provisioned, the new police force moved west as far as Roche Percee where they had to break off horses and men who were sick from the harsh conditions. The sick were sent north to Fort Edmonton, while the rest continued their march west to the mountains. Sam's job was to get the sick to Edmonton, a trip that was over a thousand kilometres and took two and a half difficult months to complete. Towards the end of the trek, failing horses had to be lifted over rough parts on two poles, a man in front, a man behind.

South of the *Medicine Line*, Sitting Bull's well-armed Sioux killed General Custer and his men in the battle of Little Big Horn. Sam and his men were brought down to Fort Macleod to face the possibility that Sitting Bull would escape into Canada and bring his people with him. When Sam's three year contract came to an end, he was offered a commission if he would sign on for another term. They needed him. He signed.

The next years were taken up with theft, liquor salesmen, settlers and the challenge of feeding Sitting Bull's Sioux who had indeed come to Canada. Sam continued to police with unwavering justice and tolerance. He was promoted to Inspector.

A blanket, owned by a dying white man, was brought up the Mississippi on a paddle-wheeler and sold to an aboriginal man. Smallpox cut the North American aboriginal population in half.

White hunters killed buffalo for their hides and left the meat to rot on the prairie. Buffalo, a major source of aboriginal food, disappeared.

In the Cypress hills, on a whim, white hunters killed a family of sixteen aboriginals.

Sitting Bull

The Cypress Hills

On April 2, 1885, Big Bear's Cree warriors killed nine men and took two female hostages at Frog Lake. Sam was assigned to the army under General Middleton and formed a group called Steele's Scouts.

Middleton didn't know how to fight aboriginals and dithered himself into inaction. Against Middleton's orders, Sam and his Scouts ended Big Bear's insurgence.

Middleton was *returned* to England and given the job of guarding the crown jewels.

Soon came the construction crews for the Canadian Pacific Railway and Sam was given the job of keeping the workers out of trouble. The rails progressed across the prairies at a speed of five miles a day. Sam had a moveable tent and a crew of men who brought offenders in for trials. Sam began to show a knack for penalty inventions that would blossom into genius as time passed.

At exactly the wrong time, an American railway completed a new line and all the gunslingers and troublemakers that followed railway construction moved north to accompany Van Horne's railway through the mountains. Van Horne asked if he could have Sam's help. Sam was promptly given British Columbia credentials and served as policeman and magistrate all the way to the final spike.

Big Bear

Sam was reassigned to the NWMP and was setting up a system of police patrols when he was asked to attend to troubles in the Kootenay region of British Columbia.

Chief Isadore of the Kootenay people was threatening trouble because his people had been assigned too little land and whites were mistrusted. Sam considered the complaints, found them valid and set to work. First he got Isadore more land from the government, then he erased the problem of distrust by finding two accused aboriginals innocent and two whites who had committed the murders guilty. In addition he went to the trouble of capturing the two whites in Fort Benton, Montana. Isadore was shaken, and his people impressed that a white had decided honestly and in favour of aboriginals.

Trust was revived.

Sam was married and had just enough down time to make three babies, when the Klondike Gold Rush of 1898 began. That event included thirty thousand individuals rushing down an untamed Yukon River, all of whom needed careful and caring supervision.

Sam was sent to solve it all.

In the spring, those who had heaved their 1,500 pounds of supplies seven miles up the mountain and proceeded to Lake Bennett, bumped once again into Sam Steele. Sam had invented a bouquet of irritating laws that slowed them down but kept them safe. On the day the ice left Lake Bennett, eight hundred boats, all Steele approved, started down the Yukon River.

There were political problems to solve as well. The United States said their property went inland from Chilkoot Pass. Canada said the border stopped at the top of Chilkoot Pass. Sam stocked the border crossing with a Maxim machine gun and a lot of supplies for cold weather. The Americans backed away as winter set in.

The crowd kept coming until there was no more room down the trail at Bennett Lake.

In the next few days, seven thousand boats went down the river through the wild waters of Miles Canyon and beyond. Only five people drowned.

With the lake left under police control, Sam went down the river to Dawson where he became magistrate, judge and a Solomon-like advisor for the community. Dawson was a new kind of gold town - no gunslingers, only people who knew they would be safer under a rule of law. Citizens learned to respect him for his fair and interesting solutions for those who broke the law: two weeks washing dishes, a month on the woodpile and even snow shovelling, until attitudes changed.

The solutions were not only friendly and fitting, they saved the town five dollars a day!

Sam left the Klondike a hero. On his departure from Dawson,
he was given a pouch of gold nuggets collected from the people of Dawson.

As his boat pulled away from the dock, a large crowd applauded
and shouted good wishes for so long, they could still be heard
when the boat was well away and around the river bend.

George Edwards

Neither the Canadian nor American governments
wanted to claim him as their own.

It's a beautiful valley. The Tulameen River starts a little run in the mountains to the west. The Pasayten flows straight north and joins the Tulameen at a spot where new settlers built the village of Princeton. The two rivers continue to amble east and become the Similkameen. In the fall, the wind brings the smell of high pines to the valley floor and aspens paint a golden coverlet. In the spring, the rivers rush to sharpen river banks and trade a gravel bar here for a sand spit there. It gives the river a new look, a different pose each year.

In the fall of 1905, a slim friendly looking fellow named George Edwards could be seen working with pick and shovel to change the course of a trickle off the river. When he was finished, he had created a small flow along the gravel bank. After a week of running, the trickle made a small pond behind Mazie's house. The cold weather came and turned the pond into a skating rink. Seven-year-old Mazie had always wanted to skate so she was thrilled. Edwards enjoyed the children. He had ridden into Princeton the preceding year (1904) and was a boarder at the Schisler place. He called himself a "southern gentleman" who needed some peace and a pleasant place to live out his old age.

He made an acceptable contribution to the community when he went hunting or drove cattle to the "coast" with the local men. His expertise as a hunter and a cattleman was noticed and appreciated. He told stories of the wild American West and ambled off every now and then to go "prospecting," a respectable profession.

If he wasn't out somewhere in the summer, you could find him with his horse, a beautiful white animal named "Pat." George curried and groomed Pat and when he was as beautiful as George could make him, he walked Pat to town where the kids would come running for...

" A free ride. A free ride,"
he'd call,
"for all who want to ride
the amazing white horse
who can tell time!"

To prove his claim,

Mr. Edwards would pull out
his pocket watch,
squint at it as though he
couldn't see it, then
show the horse the watch.

He was caught and sent to prison for the Wells Fargo job. He escaped, was again caught and sent off to San Quentin maximum-security prison. These were just his first of four visits to prison. George became an expert at escaping but the authorities were expert at catching him. Every time he escaped he was caught. By the time it was all over, George had spent more time in San Quentin than he had spent out of San Quentin. Some prison time was spent in solitary confinement where severe beatings were common.

it was no wonder George looked at the peaceful valley that held the town of Princeton as a good place to live out his days. His retirement amongst these gentle folks would have been successful for everyone if he had indeed retired. His trips to the bush for *prospecting* turned out to be a search for gold carried by trains, rather than gold in the ground. On one such adventure in May 1906, Mr. Edwards and his gang took over a C.P. R. train out of Kamloops. The adventure netted the gang a total of $15. In spite of the tiny amount stolen, the robbery again cost Mr. Edwards his freedom. On this occasion a great deal of public sentiment was stirred up on George's behalf. "He just steals a little money from the C.P. R. every two years," they shouted. "The C.P. R. steals money from us every day."

The people of Princeton had trouble believing their Mr. Edwards robbed trains. As they gathered the details of the robbery however, they recognized his distinctive gentle manner in the "Hands up please" and the "Go safely" and "Take care" he implored his victims, as he left with their valuables.

For the Kamloops robbery, George Edwards was sent to a prison in New Westminster, B.C.

The story of the robbery, capture and subsequent escape is fascinating. It is alleged by some that feelings towards George had softened to the point where the guards had turned in his favour. One night a corner of the fence was mysteriously lifted and George limped away on his last "escape." George Edwards died as Bill Miner. His gravestone in the prison town of Milledgeville, Georgia reads, "The last of the western bandits."

Pat would stomp his hoof the correct number of times to match the hour. The parents laughed, the children were amazed and gradually George Edwards conned his way into the trust and affection of the Princeton community.
George Edwards was not George Edwards.

George was born Billy Macdonald but he dumped that name for three or four others he would use as need dictated. Depending on where he was, Billy Macdonald was William Morgan, William Miner or George Edwards. His upbringing was less than gentlemanly. He received a formal education from two grandmothers, one Roman Catholic and one Protestant and left their care at fifteen. At sixteen, George led a gang of rowdies who took $75,000 from the Wells Fargo Express. For that and a continual run of other crimes, he was placed on the Wells Fargo most wanted list. For the train robberies in his collection of crimes, George was sought after continually by the famous detective agency, Pinkerton.

The Boy in White Shorts

I had chosen a park bench to warm my bottom and
sort my thoughts. The bench across from mine
became occupied by a mother and her little boy.
I didn't know his name. It was early fall. Mother
became engrossed in her newspaper and the little boy,
cute and three or four years old, circled his mother's bench
collecting leaves. He took his time to make the decision
of whether a leaf was more yellow than red or more brown
than green. He placed them with great care on a curb,
according to their colour: green, red, orange, yellow and
brown. Each meticulous pile was separated from the other
by six inches of gray cement. When he had what he
considered to be enough, he stood back, hands on hips
and admired his work. Mother read.

Then he ate the red pile.

Robert Salts

On the night of February 4th 1880, the Donnelly family was murdered and their homestead burned to the ground by the Vigilance Committee of the Cedar Swamp Schoolhouse. The history of the murders is well known locally and the property on which the murders took place was not easy to sell. Robert Salts, who had a new job in a nearby school, bought it for a reasonable price. He didn't believe in ghosts.

By 2008, only corner boulders marked the shape of the burned-out homesteaders' cabin. A few feet to the west of the boulders, a newer house was built. The barn that stands a short distance behind the house is the original Donnelly barn.

Mr. Salts says he has been wakened on two separate occasions by the murdered Mrs. Donnelly who warned him of fire in his house. The fires although small, turned out to be real.

Mr. Salt's young son Charles told a coherent story of playing with the long dead Donnelly children in his upstairs bedroom. When a TV investigative team headed up to look at the bedroom, the reporter was stopped halfway, "by a solid pressure against my chest." The barn has exhibited a variety of apparitions with reasonable frequency.

Jerry Potts

A wandering "half and half" Blackfoot
seemed an easy target.

There was a knock on the trader's door. Jerry's father went to it and opened the small window in the top. The man on the outside pulled the trigger and the bullet went through Mr. Potts' forehead killing him instantly. The whole thing was a mistake. The Peigan man who did the shooting had been told he could not trade at the post until he sobered up. His feelings were hurt and he wanted revenge for the slight. He fired through the door thinking the man who had turned him away was inside. Instead it was the kindly Mr. Potts, Jerry's dad.

After a time, Jerry's mother (a Blood Indian) married a new man, a Scot trader named Alexander Harvey with a vile temper and a bad reputation. He often expressed his bad temper by beating Jerry. His beatings changed Jerry from a rambunctious child into a quiet boy who for the rest of his life, chose to speak infrequently. Jerry ran away and was soon adopted by another Scots trader named Andrew Dawson. Andrew Dawson wasn't going to let this quiet young man sit around. By the time Jerry was ready to go out on his own, Mr. Dawson had seen to it that Jerry was properly schooled, knew the trading business and could speak the languages of all the aboriginal peoples of the region.

The western prairie was Jerry's love. The land was free of roads and fences; all you needed was a horse and a rifle and you could live off the land. There was no one to say, "that's mine" or "you can't go there." Jerry travelled everywhere. He explored the land until no other man knew the landscape as well as Jerry.

Jerry's appearance became rough and disheveled but inside was a balanced and intelligent man who often hid behind his silence and rough exterior. When it suited the occasion, he dressed in the clothes of the white man. Sometimes it suited him to wear the clothes of the aboriginal but most often he dressed half and half in the buckskin leggings and moccasins of the Blackfoot and the waistcoat and fedora of the white.

Jerry wasn't pretty. He spoke seldom and rode a horse like he was a part of the animal.

Jerry lived a very free and easy life but it was also full of dangers. The Cree and the Assinaboine who lived in the northern part of Alberta and the northwestern part of Saskatchewan probed the land of the Blackfoot continually to find a weak spot or a stray. The Crow and the Sioux tested them from the south and the Kootneys made occasional forays to the east out of Kicking Horse Pass. A wandering "half and half" Blackfoot seemed an easy target.

Ambling along one day looking for buffalo, Jerry was suddenly surrounded by seven Crow warriors. Three had bows and arrows and four had rifles. They decided not to kill him right away and invited him to their encampment to meet their chief.

Jerry did not have an option so he accepted with a smile. As they started off, the rifle-carrying warriors rode behind and the men with bows in front; Jerry listened as they discussed how to kill him. The Crow spoke in their own tongue and didn't know Jerry could understand. When Jerry heard the sound of a rifle being cocked, he threw himself from his horse and landed on one knee with a revolver ready in his hand. The leader of the group got a shot away that yanked at Jerry's shirt. Jerry shot the four men behind him where they stood. The three men in front ran for their lives. Jerry raced away to gather warriors of his own.

In the evening, the Blackfoot he had collected, attacked the Crow camp leaving many dead and wounded. A few were left alive to tell the story of the amazing "half and half" who could not be killed. Jerry said a smart warrior always left a few live ones to tell the story of his exploits.

Jerry kept in touch with his mother who had left the violent Mr. Harvey and gone to live with a community of Blackfoot. One of the Blackfoot chiefs took Jerry with him to wage war against the Cree. Jerry's skill and courage cemented a life-long friendship.

The Blackfoot chief called Crowfoot became a legendary leader of the Blackfoot Nation, distinguishing himself as a great leader with both his own people and the whites.

Crowfoot

The aboriginal discovered liquor the way a rock band discovers drugs. Once they'd experienced the rush, they cared for nothing but another bottle. The beautiful bodies of active outdoor men softened and became unattractive. Decorative clothing was sold to pay for liquor, men and women shuffled about in rags. At Calgary, a trader reported seventy violent deaths in one year from whiskey-induced fights. Families were destroyed.

The main source of spirits was the whiskey trader. To service the Blackfoot Nation, a group from Fort Benton in Montana, built a place of business in the center of the Blackfoot Nation at the confluence of the St. Mary and the Oldman Rivers. They called the place Fort "Whoop-up."

Jerry's friend Crowfoot was distraught about the condition and the future of his people. It was time for a police force to limit the liquor supply and offer a system of rules that would be equally enforced for both aboriginal and white.

Prime Minister John A. MacDonald (who also had a little trouble with the bottle from time to time) saw the need and sent the newly organized North West Mounted Police west through the summer of 1874.

The N.W.M.P. found they needed someone who knew the country well so they asked around and were directed to Jerry Potts. They hired Jerry as their guide and interpreter.

When this sort of military insertion was tried in the United States, it often ended in failure, deaths and permanent hostilities. Because of the very obvious deterioration of his people, Crowfoot was willing to talk about the advantages a police force might have to contain the decay of his Blackfoot Nation.

Once again Jerry Potts played an important part. He was equally conversant in English and the many aboriginal languages. Because of his friendship with Crowfoot and a growing trust in Col. McLeod of the N.W.M.P., he was right in the middle where he could do the most good. Jerry told Crowfoot of Col. McLeod's needs and feelings, and Col. McLeod what Crowfoot was thinking.

Col. McLeod

Consequently, talks between the two men came to an amicable agreement very quickly. Jerry kept the two men informed and traveled widely amongst the aboriginals to convince them the new police were an answer for their difficulties. Jerry worked for the Mounted Police for the rest of his life.

Jerry was happily married to two sisters, Panther Woman and Spotted Killer. In his later years, he married a woman named Long Time Laying Down. He had many children and it was agreed at his death that he was a wise and able friend and no man was ever his equal as a guide.

Robert Hampton Gray

Captain Ruck-Keene of the aircraft carrier *Formidable* knew a conclusion to the war was near and asked his air commanders to tell the pilots to avoid unnecessary risks. However, when men have spent all their young lives in training to be warriors and are in a battle with people who want to kill them, "avoiding risk" did not make a lot of sense. Everything they did involved risk.

At 9.25 A.M. on June 9 1945, Flight Commander Hampton Gray noted Japanese destroyers at anchor in Onagawa Bay.

His two flights of Corsairs were on their way to shorten the airfield at Matsushima, Japan. Hammy tucked the information about the destroyers in the back of his mind and flew on.

World War II had only five days left to go. The Corsairs had taken off in early light from the deck of the British aircraft carrier Formidable. Each aircraft was armed with two 500-pound bombs tucked under its wings.

For the most part, Hammy grew up in Nelson, British Columbia. As a young adult, he enrolled at U.B.C. and became editor of the yearbook and a member of the Student Peace Movement. As the German blitzkrieg smashed through Poland and into Western Europe, Hammy changed his mind about peace. He and two friends drove to Calgary and signed up at the naval station on the prairie, *HMCS Tecumseh*.

After a time as a sailor in training, Hammy switched from ships to planes and began what seemed a never-ending stream of training sessions. At first, he had to take a course on how to, then he had to take two courses on how to do it better.

Hammy was trained to fly Fairey Battle Trainers, Hurricanes and a Walrus. Then he was sent to inactive places like Kenya where he learned to fly other aircraft - Swordfish, Wildcats and Fulmars. Hammy had lost a cousin and a brother in battle and he didn't want to train any more. He began to worry the war would end and he would be a very well trained pilot who never quite managed to fight. Following four long years of training in June 1944, Hammy was assigned to the carrier *HMS Formidable*.

On July 14, the *Formidable* sailed north, its designated target, the German battleship *Tirpitz* that was holed up in a Norwegian fjord.

A German submarine warned the *Tirpitz* that the *Formidable* was on its way, so it was well prepared. German destroyers, shore batteries and the augmented armament of the *Tirpitz* made its defensive position very tough to break. Hammy's job was to strafe flak positions on the shore and draw fire away from the Barracudas who were bombing the *Tirpitz*. In the end, Hammy's group achieved their objective. The squadron strafed and bombed the local airport, the wharfs, and executed a daring low-level attack on three German destroyers.

Hammy's courage was recognized with a "Mention in Dispatches for undaunted courage and skill." When film from the gun cameras was reviewed, another characteristic of Hammy Gray came to light. The normal footage showed the German sailors running for cover. Hammy's gun camera showed the expressions on their faces.

In April 1945, the *Formidable* was assigned to join *Indefatigable, Victorious, Illustrious, Indomitable* and *Implacable* as members of the British Pacific Fleet. The British Fleet was to move under the overall command of the U.S. Navy. The huge entourage, the largest collection of aircraft carriers in history, sailed up the western Pacific towards Japan with obvious intentions. Carrier planes took off to harass Japanese shipping and airfields along the coast. Hammy was a Canadian on a British ship in an American strike force on its way to end the war.

On the day Hammy spotted Japanese destroyers in Onagawa Bay, the Japanese defenders also saw Hammy's two flights of Corsairs and decided they should be prepared in case the Corsairs came back. The 1000-ton destroyer escort *Amakusa* was warned and defenses on the ships and around the shore were manned. The *Amakusa* was one of three destroyers in the bay; a second destroyer was the brand new *Ohama*; the third was the *Soya*. The *Ohama* and its sister ship *Soya*, had recently had their considerable armament removed and placed along the shore of the bay. *Minesweeper #33* commanded by LCDR Takeo Kojima carried an armament of six anti-aircraft cannons and a cluster of machine guns. The *Amakusa* was armed with nine anti-aircraft cannons and three large guns.

Around the bay, other craft, all members of the Onagawa Defense Squadron, prepared to defend Onagawa Bay. *Subchasers 1,3,6* and *42, Minesweepers 1,3,* and *4*, and the minesweeper *Kongo Maru* were ready. The *Amakusa* raised anchor and moved to a more protected position near the shore. *Minesweeper 33* moved to a shallow portion of the bay where she could be easily raised if she was sunk. Defenses were on their toes and Japanese sailors were good marksmen. Hammy took a look at the airport at *Matsushima*, saw that it was badly damaged by other attackers and made the decision to go for the destroyers. He assumed his best chance at surprise was to go inland behind Onagawa and approach the bay from behind the hills. From 10,000 feet, he dove down into the protection of the hills and popped out into the bay. From there he flew in the open for thirty seconds before reaching the *Amakusa*. .

In their assessment of how an enemy would attack, the Japanese had foreseen exactly this scenario. All the shore batteries, the ships and the Amakusa were waiting for this attack. The air was filled with cannon and machine gun fire, each gunner trying to shoot down the lead Corsair. The Corsair was hit almost immediately and began to show flames from the engine cover. Shells smashed into the aircraft. We don't know if Hammy was hit at this point; we do know that the volume of fire was enough to suggest to Hammy that he did not have the advantage of surprise and he should quit.

Hammy did not quit. His training and experience had taught him the only way to sink a target was a smooth, calm and unwavering approach. At fifty feet from the surface of the bay, the Corsair was an easy target. Hammy continued. Cannon fire shook his craft; the bomb on his left wing was shot from its mount. Steady flight for four more seconds gave Hammy his run-in. At exactly the right moment, he released his remaining bomb. The bomb smashed through the deck, entered the engine room and ignited the ammunition magazine. The *Amakusa* capsized and went to the bottom in seconds.

Every gunner in the bay had done his best to shoot the aircraft down. A pigeon could not have flown through the rain of fire. The Corsair spit parts and pieces, a long plume of flame trailed behind.

Hammy had stayed in control just long enough to drop his bomb in the right spot but he was probably dead by the time he cleared the ship.

The Corsair rotated, obviously now without control and crashed upside down into Onagawa Bay.

Hammy's mates were stunned by their loss. He had always been an enjoyable and easy going friend as well as a competent commander. Throughout that afternoon and the morning of the next day, the pilots returned to Onagawa Bay where every Japanese ship was sunk and every allied aircraft in the attack received damage.

Robert Hampton Gray was posthumously awarded the Victoria Cross. He was the last Canadian to die on operations in the Second World War.

In an act of amazing generosity, the Japanese men who fought against him that day, erected a monument on the shores of Onagawa Bay to recognize his unusual courage and determination.

Robert
Hampton Gray

Distinguished Service Cross   Victoria Cross

When the author spoke to Hammy's sister to confirm some of these facts, he asked if she thought of her brother as a hero.

She replied, "Yes, I do, but not as much a hero as my father. He was the one who had to tell my mother her remaining son was dead."

For those who are interested in airplanes, these are the aircraft Hammy learned to fly.

Walrus

Hurricane

Swordfish

Hellcat

Fairey Fulmer

Tom Three Persons

Cyclone had never been beaten.

Cyclone was a magnificent stallion, black from nose to tail. Tom Three Persons was glad he pulled his name from the draw because Cyclone was the best way to win the competition at the Calgary Stampede. The stallion had thrown one hundred and twenty-seven riders in the past seven years and had never in his life been ridden to a standstill. A rider's chance of staying aboard the ferocious animal was slim.

When Tom Three Persons got on Cyclone, the horse could feel he had a rider who knew his business; the seat was certain, the knees were strong. When the chute swung open, he knew he had to do his best.

He arrived in the ring in one mighty back-arching leap. That didn't work so he threw himself in the air as high as he could and landed stiff-legged to rattle Tom's teeth. Two more of those and Tom was still with him. Tom ran his spurs up the stallion's chest and down his flank to let him know he was still on tight. Cyclone left the ground facing one way and landed facing the opposite way. He slammed Tom into the fence to try to rub him off and gaining little, reared straight up threatening to fall over backwards. Tom didn't buy it, he stuck like glue. Cyclone had done his best and still had the weight of the man on his back. He gave a half-hearted kick in the air and broke into a gallop.

The crowd went wild.

Cyclone's efforts gave Tom the bronc riding trophy for the Calgary Stampede and permanent residence in the Canadian Rodeo's Hall of Fame.

Andrew George Latta McNaughton

Four hundred miles of defensive trenches, layer behind layer, stretched from the top of France to the bottom. By 1916, the line between the Germans and the British, French and Belgian armies extended from Ypre in the north of France, southward through Lille, Lens, Vimy, Arras and St. Quentin to Reims, east to Verdun, down to St. Mihiel and in a sweeping arc, south to the Swiss border near Bern.

On the north end of the line, a five-hundred-foot bump known as Vimy Ridge had been made into an impregnable defensive position by the Germans. The French had sent twenty divisions against the ridge and lost 150,000 soldiers. The British had thrown themselves against the ridge several times with the same number of casualties. On January 19 1917, because he had no other reasonable choice, the Commanding Officer of the British Army declared that in the coming spring offensive, only four divisions of Canadian troops would be expected to defeat the German defenses on Vimy Ridge.

Byng

An English officer named Julian Byng was made the commanding officer of the Canadian troops. He was so appreciated by Canadians for his knowledge and wisdom that many years later he was made Canada's Governor General. Byng did not tolerate pretensions, politics or the inability of his command structures to create new tactics. He studied his choices well, he reached into his bag of Canadian officers and pulled out a twenty-seven-year-old engineering professor from McGill named Andrew McNaughton.

Mr. McNaughton was given the responsibility of producing a successful plan for Canadian artillery. A second man with battle experience, Arthur Currie, was yanked from other duties and told to meet with the commanders of the French armies to study the battles of the Somme and Verdun. Byng was not

afraid to study past mistakes, and wanted a report on how to correct mistakes committed in those two battles.

McNaughton, who had rescued a tiger cub from a British zoo and kept it under his desk, changed the outcome of the war. He gathered a group of inventive young scientists around him and challenged them to make Canadian artillery the best in the world. The "McNaughton Club" invented a system of sight and sound-ranging that could pinpoint the position of hidden enemy guns within twenty-five feet. In a very short time, they invented systems for reading gun muzzle velocity, barrel wear and the effects of wind, temperature and humidity on the accuracy of the different kinds of artillery, thereby solving the problem of death by friendly fire. They invented a way to make Germans think their own artillery was shooting them in the back. McNaughton knew, because of the attitudes toward colonial Canadians, the *Club's* improvements would be diminished. A stuffy English General remarked, "You're taking all the fun out of war."

McNaughton

Currie produced his report, Byng and his commanders planned ways to deceive the enemy and mount an effective attack. The finished Canadian plan was not accepted by the experienced English commanders and rejected by the French. Interestingly, the Germans were aware of the Canadian soldier's ability. They put out a leaflet that told their men, "Watch out for the Canadians, they are good soldiers and under no condition will they ever desert." Part of Byng's elaborate plan of attack was to discourage and confuse the Germans before the all-out attack. In the days before the attack, 275,000 shells were dropped on the German positions. In the rear, intersecting German roads received 300,000 machine gun rounds every night. German troops called it the "week of suffering."

On April 9th at 5.30 in the morning, 983 Canadian guns with shells that varied from eighteen pounds to three hundred pounds, opened fire. Men of the four Canadian regiments crawled forward to snuggle up to the line where the accurate rolling barrage would begin.

One third of the artillery hammered the German trenches, two thirds participated in the rolling barrage. A rolling barrage is a maneuver in which artillery guns drop shells on a line that moves just ahead of their own men. It keeps the enemy huddled in his trench and unable to deal with the advancing force. Of the 84,000 Canadians who charged forward, 3,598 were killed and 7,004 were wounded. As anticipated, the earth was ripped to dust. Places the soldiers used to orient themselves, disappeared. A soldier lost in the battle asked a scout where the town of Les Tilleuls was and was told "You're standing in the middle of it." Scouts wore green armbands; mopping-up parties wore white armbands, carrying parties wore yellow and communication runners wore red. Each soldier knew where he was to go, when and where he was to stop and rest and when he was going to get where he was going. The Germans were overwhelmed and eager to surrender. A red-hot steel roof of artillery looped over the battlefield. Thousands of rounds of machine-gun fire skimmed the heads of the advancing troops.

Above these two layers, Billy Bishop and his companion flyers flew back and forth collecting signals from the battlefield.

At the end of thirty-five minutes of fighting, the Canadian troops had smashed through the first three lines of German trenches and by noon the Germans were in full retreat.

Since April 9 1917, no one has questioned the courage and ability of the Canadian soldier.

John George Brown

He backed up toward the tree, wedged the arrow that protruded from his back into a crack and threw himself forward. The arrow stayed with the tree. Mr. Brown examined the arrow and with relief found the arrowhead still attached. He poured turpentine into the wound and took it easy for a few days until he could declare himself fixed.

John George or "Kootenai" Brown was a tough nut. He served with the British army in India, in General Custer's army as a scout, as a pony express rider and a hunter. He ended up in the Waterton Lakes region of Alberta and was instrumental in having the area declared Canada's first International Park. Kootenai was made the park's first superintendent in 1911 and worked hard at keeping the area safe and available to those who love the out-of-doors.

There are only two roads in Waterton Lakes National Park. One goes to the town site and a short appendage goes up the hill to Cameron Lake.

Waterton is a hiker's park; the two roads are there to access the heads of the walking trails.

The trails are varied. The hike from Cameron Lake has a long and a short walk and gives you a good look at the lake and the Cameron Glacier above it. A climb to the Rowe Lakes takes you to two lakes, one five hundred feet directly above the other with a waterfall that joins the two. The bottom lake freezes to the bottom in winter, eliminating fish. The Rowe Lake trail has an extension that can extend your walk for two days if you wish and pop you out at Red Rock Canyon.

Across the lake from the town of Waterton, a long walk along scree slopes past Hell Roaring Canyon, culminates in a trail that appears to peter out at a cliff. If the hiker looks carefully, he will see a short climb will take him to a small tunnel. Hikers are advised to check the tunnel for occupants before they proceed on hands and knees through the tunnel to the exit.

The tunnel's exit is a hole in a flat, sheer face of high cliff. There is a steel rod on the left for a handhold and a six-inch ledge for the hiker's feet. If there is a guide, he will say, "Don't lean into the mountain and don't look down." This exhilarating walk takes the hiker to a stream that leads him to Crypt Lake. Crypt Lake is surrounded by a perfect, high walled amphitheater. The Lake is in Canada and the south wall is in Glacier National Park, U.S.A.

Not as much snow falls in the winter as used to. In the old days, the snow was so deep, the two storied hotel on the main street closed the entrance on the main floor and everyone entered through the upstairs windows. A larger and more beautiful hotel was built on a hill at the Canadian end of Waterton Lake.

During the Second World War, a spy fleeing for his life, booked a room but did not check out in the morning. He had stolen a boat and gone down the lake to the then neutral United States.

Kootenai Brown's park favours the comforts and enjoyment of people who like to walk in the out-of-doors. Cameron Lake is high in the mountains and a few miles west of the town of Waterton. Two trails, one short and one for those with stronger legs, leave from the parking lot at Cameron Lake and amble back to town.

A person with sharp eyesight can just make out a monument of stones on top of the flat-topped mountain on the western side of the lake. The monument marks the spot where the borders of British Columbia, Alberta and the U.S.A. come together.

The stream that exits Cameron Lake runs downstream to Waterton and creates an attractive fifty-foot fall of water as it enters the town.

Ethel Catherwood

A tall young woman from Saskatchewan entered the 1928 Amsterdam Olympics in the first year in which women were allowed to compete. The crowd responded to her grace and beauty by nicknaming her "Saskatoon Lily." She won the high jump competition, a gold medal and a three thousand dollar prize. The prize, she said, would be used to continue her studies in piano.

A Stony Chief

The young man travelled as fast as he could but still arrived late for his appointment with the chief of the Stony First Nations near Seebe, Alberta. When questioned, the young woman at the front desk said, "I'm very sorry sir, the Chief has gone for a walk." The man asked if he might wait until the Chief returned. After a brief pause she replied, "He said he might be back by the end of the week."

Wilfred Thomas Grenfell

Quietly and carefully he rolled his beloved Moody over onto its back and drove the knife into his heart. The speed of his action did not ease the ache that engulfed him or protect him from a sudden slash of the dog's teeth.

Continuing, he received a second bite from Sue and a few minutes later, Spy succumbed freely and without complaint to the sentence bestowed upon him by his master.

Their master, Wilfred Grenfell stood and studied the ice to see if his exertions had caused any damage. It wasn't real ice; it was very fragile slob ice, a frozen slab of slush about ten feet by twelve. Everything was holding together but to his horror, an off shore breeze was moving him down Hare Bay and directly out into the Atlantic Ocean.

Determined to stay alive as long as he could, he cut off the tops of his long boots and tied them over his shoulders to keep the freezing wind from his back. He then skinned the dogs to use their pelts as a dry platform and stacked their bodies as a windbreak. As the day wore on he could see the cliffs of the north shore as they slipped by but knew he was too far away to be seen and rescued. That night he lay down beside a dog named Doc and rolled up in the pelts. By morning his tiny domain was a few feet smaller and one of his hands was badly frozen. He was beginning to suffer from hunger and the cold seemed personal with its bite. The wind direction had shifted in the night and drawn him closer to the north shore of Hare Bay.

He floated past a fishing station called Ireland's Bight. He saw the shacks in the distance but reminded himself the men fished in the summer and went inland for winter. Grenfell was beginning to weaken. He saw rescuers where there were none. He saw a shadow, a splash of light that could not be a man or a boat. But then, slowly, away in the distance, something rose and fell, rose and fell. There was a boat, miles down the bay moving terribly slowly, but it was indeed coming for him.

The day before, George Davis had seen Grenfell, a tiny black dot riding a tiny white dot. Together he and George Reid confirmed their find with Mr. Reid's telescope. They got going before sun up. George Davis manned one oar, George Andrews another, George Reid and his son manned the remaining two. They pushed, pulled, lifted and rowed until they reached Grenfell's tiny floe.

When they were close enough to see him, they broke into tears. Their cherished Doctor Grenfell was barely recognizable. Dehydration gave him the appearance of a much older man. Hunger bowed him and the hands he had used to sew, salve and save so many lives, could not move.

A team of nine dogs had come up to St. Anthony's, from Canada Bay to take the doctor to a man whose leg had become dangerously infected. It was decided the nine-dog team was too tired to leave on a return trip right away. Grenfell, not wanting to delay, packed a komatik with dressings and medicine and headed out behind a team of his own seven dogs. As usual he was full of energy, enthusiasm and confidence in his ability to make the trip alone. He pushed along quickly, reached Lock's Cove and stayed the night with friends. In the morning, his options were to cut across the inside corner of Hare's Bay or fight the ups and downs of the shore around the bay. The ice had been firm so he took the shorter route and got to within a short distance of the south shore when conditions suddenly changed.

He realized he was no longer walking on ice but a kind of deep "sish" or slush. The wind had come up and parted the ice. His komatik began to sink so to keep the dogs from being pulled down, he cut the traces. Still hoping he could reach the shore, he and the dogs plunged forward. The first piece of harder ice they landed on began to sink. After several tries, he got the dogs to switch to a chunk of slush. It had looked solid enough but it immediately separated and began to float towards the open Atlantic Ocean.

Wilfred Grenfell attended the London College Medical Hospital to earn his stripes as a doctor. He was irrepressible in all his activities and had been brought up under a Victorian code of moral manliness. The two keys to manhood were strength and athleticism. Wilf carried the sixteen pound throwing hammer around and avidly contributed to everything athletic whether he was good at it or not. For his first job as a doctor, he accepted the position of Physician for the Mission to Deep Sea Fishermen. The MDSF took care of the health and spiritual needs of fishermen in the North Sea.

Wilf knew he was needed and he revelled in helping to improve the lives of the fishermen.

To the fishermen, he showed himself to be an able professional with strength and stamina enough for two men and an infectious vitality that drew everyone to him. Wilf's spiritual beliefs were described as "wholehearted and less than intellectual."

The MDSF became aware of the needs of the Newfoundland and Labrador fishermen who worked up and down the coasts of Eastern Canada and sent Wilf to investigate. Wilf arrived in St. John's, Newfoundland the day the entire city burned to the ground. The ship he arrived in was turned into a medical station for the wounded. Wilf took on duties in Newfoundland with his usual energy. Because of his efforts, small hospitals appeared on the coasts of Labrador and Newfoundland. First one ship and then three ships provided medical assistance. When an MDSF ship pulled into harbour, boats, ships and small craft with endless people who had medical needs, immediately surrounded them.

In the summer of 1892, Dr. Grenfell himself saw over nine hundred people. The fishermen and their families loved him and appreciated his efforts on their behalf.

After a few years and because of the efforts of Wilf and the MDSF, people's medical needs were a little better cared for. They were still however, living in dreadful poverty. Under-housed, under-clothed and too often hungry, they had to continue (in their words) to "work or die." The MDSF ships carried a limited amount of food and clothing to dispense where the need seemed greatest. It was evident however, something much more was required. Seeing what his efforts had accomplished and what they had not, Wilfred Thomas Grenfell's medical and spiritual mission began to include efforts towards the social and financial betterment of Newfoundland fishermen.

The fishing families worked within a system imposed on them by the merchants of St. John's. The merchant supplied the fisherman with his needs for the summer and when the fisherman returned in the fall, the merchant was paid in fish. There was no money involved and the system was easily manipulated to the merchant's benefit. It did not matter how many fish were brought to pay the bill, the merchant made that amount exactly the cost of the supplies the fisherman had taken in the spring. Fishermen could not get ahead.

Wilf got the fishermen together, helped them to organize cooperatives and to eventually replace the merchants.

When he returned to St. Anthony in November of 1894, Wilf was applauded for a trip during which he visited every family on the Labrador Coast. He had gone from Blanc Sablon on the southeast corner, to Home Island, one thousand miles north on the farthest tip of the Labrador Peninsula. Wilf and the other doctors, now members of Grenfell's team, saw over three thousand patients in the twelfth year of MDSF operations. Dr. Grenfell, in addition to his medical duties, oversaw the construction of a new sawmill, a fox farm and fulfilled duties as magistrate.

Not everyone was happy with Wilf Grenfell. In St. John's, the Church of England's bishop, Rev. L. Jones, was deeply jealous of Wilf's popularity. The Roman Catholic hierarchy complained only a little less. The merchants were furious over their loss of control. In late 1800, St. John's was not a pretty

ction

---

place. Politicians stayed in power with blatant patronage. An unshakable caste system held the rich and powerful firmly in place.

The powerful dispersed false rumors.

Newspapers supported the status quo, "Don't give those fishermen help, they will become dependent and we'll have to support them for the rest of their lives." Rumour had it that Grenfell was working for money. That was true; Wilf Grenfell was working hard for money.

Through the winter months, he travelled to Halifax and spoke at Dalhousie University. He fascinated crowds in New Brunswick, Montreal, Toronto, Boston, Chicago, New York and as far away as Victoria.

He enlisted the help of a young William Lyon Mackenzie King. Franklin Delano Roosevelt offered generous support. Andrew Carnegie donated libraries. Volunteers, doctors and money poured east to the benefit of Newfoundland and Labrador fishermen.

Doc

The Boy

The shop owners in the tiny Saskatchewan town still saw him as a boy because he was open, well mannered and genial. His appearance belied his boyhood. The shoulders were well formed and had a job holding up arms, grown large with work on the farm.

The *boy* finished his purchases and walked onto the boardwalk that protected the townspeople from the muddy street. The man walking towards him had a revolver in a holster on his hip. As they were about to pass, the man suddenly stepped in front of the boy and said, "You! This is my boardwalk, you walk in the mud." Before the gunslinger could think to move, the boy stepped forward, grabbed a shirtfront in one hand and the gunslinger's pants in the other, raised him over his head and threw him off the boardwalk into the mud.

Legend says that the gunslinger was Billy the Kid and from that day forward they described the encounter as the day, "The Boy met the Kid."

Deerfoot

The race took place on the open prairie near Calgary. Deerfoot ran against a Blackfoot runner and a travelling professional from Great Britain named James Green. Calgarians were not surprised when Deerfoot won the eighty-five mile race.

Two years later in 1886, Deerfoot ran a ten mile race against J.W. Stokes of Birmingham, England and a Winnipeg runner named George Irvine. Again Deerfoot came in first but Mr. Stokes complained that the locals had an advantage when they ran in countryside they were familiar with. Deerfoot shrugged and with a little hesitation, agreed to re-run the race on a local track. Deerfoot had never run on a manicured track before and was hesitant to start. He watched the runner from Birmingham complete six full laps to make sure there wasn't anything funny going on, then stepped onto the track and began to run. Mr. Stokes was surprised to see his opponent run past him seven times.

Deerfoot was an aboriginal runner, much appreciated in the days before the telegraph when he was the fastest way to transfer news from tribe to tribe. To show their appreciation for Deerfoot's abilities, Calgarians named the fastest way to get through the city, "Deerfoot Trail."

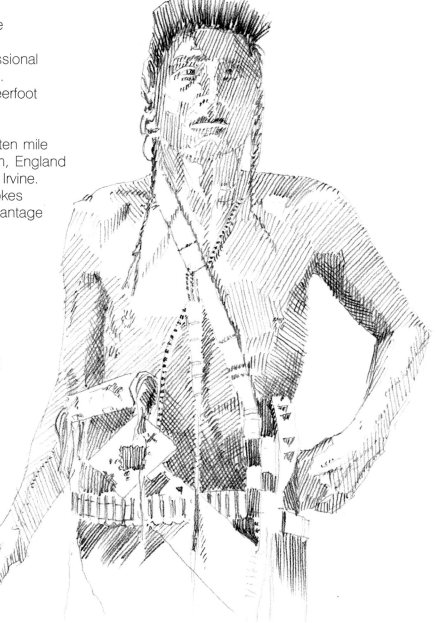

Alexander Mackenzie

Half way there and from a vantage point
above the river, Mackenzie stood amazed.
North to south, as far as he could see,
there were majestic snow topped mountains,
one after the other, like the spine of the world.

The trip was, in Alexander's mind, a complete failure. He had already fought his way up the river that went all the way to the Arctic Ocean. It did not provide him with much in the way of a new trade route and it did not take him to the Pacific Ocean.

He had returned to his starting place at Lake Athabaska and was now trying to find the Pacific by going south and west.

The old man of the Beaver tribe told him the height of land was eight hundred and seventeen paces past the first little lake at the end of the Peace River. "The best way up the river is to keep right, stay on the Peace. Don't take the left turn at Smokey River." So he and his men struggled through the tricks and traps of the Peace and up into the mountains.

The climb up the raging Peace had worn everyone thin. Canoes were walked in the water and pulled with ropes from the top of cliffs that lined the canyons. Canoes smashed and tipped, provisions were lost and food supplies ran short. They persisted and finally followed the river to a point where it became an insignificant trickle. The men struggled farther into the narrow gap between two mountains. A thick underbrush of thorn and deadfall opened to tall thin pines. They stopped climbing. The walk became a pleasure as they passed one small lake and proceeded along a portage. A man began to count paces, " five, six, seven." After half a mile when the count got to "eight hundred and nine, eight hundred and ten," the pines opened to reveal a small lake. Baskets and packages hung in the trees like parcels for Christmas.

Alexander Mackenzie was elated. The packages identified this place as an important terminus for traveling aboriginal bands. The terminus was the height of land. This was where all waters began to flow west. All he had to do now was follow one of them to the Pacific. They took some hooks and a net from the hanging packages and in return, left a knife, some fire-steels and an awl.

Alexander was the first non-aboriginal to cross the Continental Divide, the highest point of land between the Atlantic and the Pacific Oceans. This place was his door to the Pacific, but it took Alexander Mackenzie and his men a long time to navigate the impossible rivers and difficult-to-find-your-way-around mountain ranges.

In the final analysis, Alexander Mackenzie was successful because he was unlike other explorers. He could curtail his pride and admit to his own ignorance. He did not attempt to go forward without learning from the people who lived in the places that lay ahead of him.

When he reached North Bentick Arm, the friendly people of Bella Coola smiled and told him it was just a short walk to his long sought after Pacific Ocean.

The Three Sisters

A traveler to Alberta entered the Rocky Mountains and climbed slowly up the Bow Valley. He passed Grotto Mountain and other beautiful walls of stone before he reached the town of Canmore. As he entered Canmore, a glance to his left revealed a large mountain with three peaks side by side. After a heavy snow fall in 1883, a Major Rogers had named the peaks the *Three Nuns*. Because of his spiritual inclination, he named the smaller peak Faith, the middle peak Hope and the tallest Charity.

The locals didn't like a name tied to a religion; they re-named the mountain *The Three Sisters*.

Castle Mountain

To honour the success of a military leader in the Second World War, another mountain, just down the road, had its name changed from *Castle Mountain* to *Mount Eisenhower.* The locals continue to use *Castle Mountain*.

Three More Sisters

Three spinster sisters lived together in the house in which they were born near London, Ontario. The three were very happy with the way things were and never went hunting for men or trouble; they were self-sufficient and never complained. They were social, went to church, local events, political speeches and community gatherings. One day, one of the ladies expressed the desire to indulge in a vacation. The other two agreed that would be a good idea and a great discussion ensued about where they would go and how. Bus tours, sailing ships, ranch-style getaways, everything was gleefully included in their deliberations.

In the end, they decided to buy a brand new DeSoto automobile, learn to drive and do the 2,485 mile round trip to a good hotel in Florida. The trip was marvelous; they could not believe how much fun it was to visit a brand new place and use their new driving skills. They made it there and back without a driving error and bang on the budget they had chosen.

Two days after their arrival home, the youngest sister died. It was a normal and understandable passing; still the two older sisters were heart broken. They left the car untouched in the driveway where they had parked it when they returned from Florida. One evening, the oldest sister phoned a friend whose husband ran a construction company. Two days later, a construction crew removed the west wall of the living room, built a ramp and drove the DeSoto into a space next to the piano. The ramp was removed and the wall repaired. The engine was never started again while the ladies were alive. The two sisters would often sit in the car beside the piano to remember their sister and recount the stories of their happy trip.

When the remaining two sisters died, the house was sold and the car removed and sold for a good price to a man who kept vintage cars for movie sequences. He was amazed to see a car of that age with only 2498 miles on the speedometer.

Peter Pond

He was unique and had many stories. He fought with the Union Army, killed a competing fur trader in a duel, was the first white man to cross the portage La Loche into the Athabaska region and after working for several small fur companies, he became a founding member of the North West Fur Company.

He survived for years, alone in an unexplored wilderness of which whites had almost no knowledge. He worked with and listened to the native people. They drew maps in the dirt and Mr. Pond took notes of their source, drew them again in detail and passed them on to other men working in the wilds.

Mackenzie River

Lake Athabaska

Peace River

Hudson Bay

Lake Winnipeg

A rough copy of one of
Peter Pond's maps

Alexander Mackenzie and David Thompson relied on his maps to help them in their own explorations.

One of the tales Peter Pond would later tell was the day he found a sticky, flammable substance, oozing out of the layered walls of the Athapasscow (Athabaska) River.

James Morris

The *Hannah and Eliza* was a beautiful, square rigged 231-ton windjammer. Lloyds of London insured her and her competent crew under an A-1 rating.

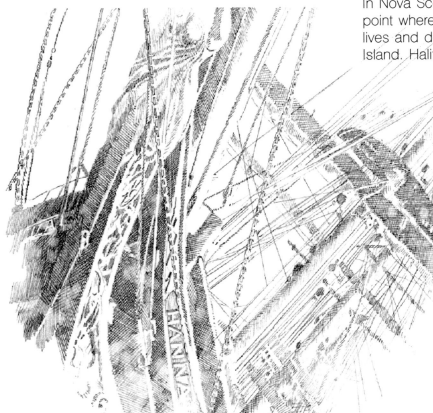

In Nova Scotia, public concern had grown to a point where something had to be done about the lives and dollars sucked into the sand on Sable Island. Halifax had become a prominent harbour and to get to Halifax ships had to make the dangerous run past Sable Island. Sailing ships were driven by wind and at times the wind drove them where they did not want to go. Hidden shoals and pounding surf circled every inch of the Island's coast. There was no harbour and no safe place to come ashore. Under the water, unseen hills of sand grew and dissipated continually. Even the part of the Island that protruded above the water became a different size and shape each year.

In 1823, Sable Island was two miles across and twenty-five miles long. In 1851, it was one mile wide and twenty-two miles long. A measurement in 1984 showed a slender strip only a half mile wide. A lighthouse built on the west end had tipped over into the sea. Forty miles north and west, a small island appeared then disappeared two years later.

The strong wind didn't care how beautiful the *Hannah and Eliza* was, it threw her onto a reef on the south side of Sable Island.

She was immoveable, and the high surf began to beat her to kindling. The crew, afraid the ship would be pulled further under, cut the masts and pushed the sails, spars and rigging overboard.

Thirteen crew members survived the sinking by fighting their way ashore. They were pleased to be on land but not very enthusiastic about the island they had landed on. This was after all, the Island of Sand, Sable Island, that had no human habitation and was known by all sailors as the graveyard of the Atlantic. Stories of ghosts, starvation and death in the cold, were commonplace.

The crew was quite startled when a man on a horse galloped down the beach and swung out of the saddle to introduce himself. The man was James Morris, superintendent of the new *Sable Island Establishment* for rescuing shipwrecked souls.

Today the island is a twenty-five mile long sand dune with two, seventy-mile long underwater arms that extend to the northwest and northeast. The entire stretch of sand sits on the edge of the Atlantic Abyss.

Fog shadows Sable, frequently and suddenly. The warm Gulf Stream flows up the west side and the cold North Atlantic current flows down the east and fog hides the Island like a blanket.

Sable's secretive and restless nature caught many ships off guard. Ships were sometimes trapped too far away from shore to be reached. An observer could only watch helplessly, aware of screams and cries for rescue, while the ship was pounded in the crashing surf. Sometimes nothing came ashore until years later when moving sands gave up a board or a bone.

Nova Scotia's House of Assembly formed a committee to select someone brave enough to live in isolation and strong enough to pull men from the sea. James Morris won the job because he had been a Royal Navy man for fourteen years and he showed, "resilience, strength, kindness and resource."

Mr. Morris, his family and a small group of helpers were deposited on Sable Island in October 1801. The *Hannah and Eliza* sailors were the first ship's crew rescued by the new Establishment. It took two years to get the survivors off the sand and back to their homes.

The Establishment grew, dormitories were constructed for larger numbers of stranded sailors. Regular patrols circled the island. A boat to take the rescuers out to unreachable wrecks was gifted to the Establishment. A rocket launcher capable of shooting a lifesaving line to ships offshore was used for the first time in 1890.

Mr. Morris and his crew were able to save many people who otherwise would have disappeared without a trace.

Radar was invented and powerful engines drove ships against the wind. Fog could no longer hide the Island made of sand.

The Establishment gradually became a few derelict buildings tipped and half buried in sand. Old wrecks still move from where they sank and reappear somewhere else.

Oil has been discovered under the sands of Sable.

Crowfoot

Crowfoot was a wealthy man,
he owned eight hundred horses,
three homes and three wives.

Present knowledge says the first inhabitants of North America came over from Mongolia by crossing the land bridge that once joined Alaska with the Asian Continent. From Alaska, they found an opening in the glacial fields that allowed them to travel south to access huge areas rich in game. Through the many years of their development, these first people established a distinct set of customs and values to guide their lives; no person who was part of a community had dominance over another; leaders led only by the power of persuasion; the whole tribe took an active part in decisions; theft and violence against tribal competitors affirmed courage; honesty was part of wisdom.

There were of course, as with all races through-out time, people who did not want to adhere to rules.

Each group of early inhabitants joined a compatible group and the groups organized themselves into nations. The nations claimed areas for their groups and defended their areas against the incursions of others.

The Blackfoot Nation claimed an area that extended from the Rocky Mountains in the west well into the present province of Saskatchewan on the east. Their northern boundary was the North Saskatchewan River and their southern boundary, the Missouri River in Montana. The tribes within the Nation were the Blackfoot, the Peigan, the Blood, the Stonies and the Sarcees.

Private names of First Nation peoples often sound humorous to those outside their culture, Stabs-by-Mistake, Crying Bear, Sitting Bull or Many Names. To the First Nations people, names were important and chosen according to a standard process. The prospective mother and father would gather with respected older warriors from their family and through the course of a few days, the old warriors would tell stories of their accomplishments. If either of the parents heard a group of words they liked either for their resonance or their meaning, they would choose them as the name for the child. This process covered the first of three or four names each person would have in their lifetime. The second name was given when children entered their less dependent years.

From a list of respected ancestral names, the person himself chose a third and often final name. This process made the tracing of First Nation people through their ancestry a very difficult job.

Packs a Knife and *Attacked Towards Home* were expecting a baby. When the little boy was born, they had the usual conference and chose as his first name *Shot Close*. As a teen *Shot Close* became *Ghost Bear* and to show respect for his father, who had been killed, *Ghost Bear* became *Packs a Knife*. A raid was planned against the Crows when *Packs a Knife* was an apprentice warrior. In the raid, young *Packs a Knife* was shot from ambush. He fell, got up and recklessly rushed to the centre of the enemy camp. For his courage and willingness to die, he was given the right to take a name from his ancestral past. He chose the name "*When Crow Indian's Big Foot was Killed.*" This for convenience sake was abbreviated to *Crowfoot*.

Then came the white man. A child rushed into camp laughing and shouting, "I saw one, I saw one! He is like a fish's belly. Ha!"

Crowfoot, who continued to show courage and intelligence, became a leader of the Blackfoot Nation. He became a very wealthy man by First Nation standards; one of a very few men who could afford one home for three wives and another home for relatives and hired men. The hired men cared for his eight hundred horses.

Crowfoot, thoughtful and intelligent, correctly recognized the intrusions of the white man as an action destructive to his people's way of life. Two thirds of the Blackfoot population were dead from the white's smallpox and many more were killing themselves with the white man's alcohol.

The first half of Crowfoot's life had been occupied by acts of physical heroism that were necessary to affirm him as a valid leader by his people's rules.

The young men refused to change. A group stole horses from their Crow enemy. The young men would not return the horses so Crowfoot replaced them from his own herd and apologized to a surprised camp of enemies.

As the buffalo diminished and his people became increasingly poor, Crowfoot gave away his herd of horses and most of his belongings to any member of the tribe who asked for assistance.

While still a boy when a friend was in trouble, he tied a knife to a pole and killed the grizzly bear that was killing his friend and when still a young man, he led men against the Cree Nations,

He was wounded six times in mortal battle but recovered to lead his people again in another war. Now this brave and wise man, in his middle and closing years, chose to spend the remaining days of his life teaching his people. There was no end to the supply of whites; the only way his people could survive was by co-existing and adhering to the white man's rules. The rules he pointed out, were much the same, except for the Theft and Violence rule. No killing or stealing would be enforced by the North West Mounted Police. The young men of the Blackfoot Nation had no way to build their wealth or prove their courage.

He continued to do so until he too became a poor man who walked instead of rode.

When he recognized his health was failing and his final days were near, Crowfoot decided to make a last try at convincing his young people to change their ways. He went to talk to each of the tribes in the Blackfoot Nation. The Peigan were camped along the South Saskatchewan, the Stonies and the Sarcees were tucked up against the mountains and the Blood were in the southern prairie.

Many of the older people appreciated his ideas but the young men could not overcome a thousand years of the thrill of theft and violence and could not quickly change to the white man's rules. In his attempt to change the habits and attitudes of his young men, Crowfoot walked and rode two hundred and fifty miles.

When Sitting Bull came to ask Crowfoot to help him fight the white, Crowfoot replied, "No, I trust the N.W.M.P. to be fair with my people."

When Riel sent his emissaries to instigate war amongst the whites, the half-white and the Blackfoot Nation, Crowfoot convinced his people to say no.

No state of hostility ever existed between the white and the Blackfoot Nation.

Two years later he was gone and the camp crier called, "Mourn your great parent, you will no longer hear his kind voice or his eloquent speech. In your distress you will no longer rush to his lodge for comfort and charities. He is no more.
No one will fill his place."

And no one did.

Laura Ingersoll

"Woman Woman!"

The forest was not asleep.

A blackcap chirped, a jay told his vehement tale, a chipmunk zipped and froze, zipped and froze.

The men had heard a wolf in the distance and had instantly become acutely aware. Two men moved to a spot where they could see more clearly down the hill toward the river. Another wolf howled. Closer. Another, across the swamp, barked. Then they could see something small and indefinite.

The *wolves* were Caughnawaga First Nations fighters who were spread through the woods to watch for intruders. A single and short howl meant someone was coming, group howls meant a larger group was approaching.

On the hill, the leader squinted his eyes. He spoke quietly to another man. "What is it, a child?" Without answering the other man signaled a companion and the two moved down the hill intent on moving around behind the intruder. Occasion-ally the two would make a forest sound to keep their companion aware of where they were.

The *child* was now in the swamp, up to its neck in muck, dragging whatever floated in a trail behind it. At the river where it bumped the bottom of the hill, the child used deadfall to move one branch at a time across the rain-bloated river. The two men were now close enough to hear the sounds of distress. When she got to the shore, she crawled on hands and knees to the bank. When she tried to stand, she cried in pain and fell back, then tried again until she was able to stand and wobble up the hill.

When she stood, the two men were near enough to touch but she had no idea they were there. They were amazed to see that what they had thought was a child was instead a woman, in pain and complete disarray. As she stumbled up the hill, the men could hear her terror and all the sounds pain forces from someone near the edge of collapse.

The sun had set and moonlight was fighting for pre-eminence when Laura reached the top of the hill. They entered a small clearing. There was the sharp click of a gun being cocked.

Laura's escorts panicked and shouted, "Woman! Woman!"

The men in the forest lowered their guns. "Woman?"

Laura had left her home in Queenston, Ontario before sunrise and almost immediately bumped into the invading American soldiers who asked her what she was doing and where she was going. She alternately used stories about a missing cow and an ailing brother to get past them. It was not reasonable, they assumed, that a woman alone could do them harm. Besides they admired this particular woman. The story was that even before the battle of Queenston Heights was over, this woman had wandered the battlefield, turning dead and mutilated men over until she finally found her husband with barely a breath left in him. They wished they had a woman like that.

The night before her impromptu trip, Laura had listened at the door while the Americans who had taken over her home, discussed plans for a surprise attack on the critical British position in the woods near Beaver Dams. She discussed warning the British with her bedridden husband. Although he was afraid of the risk in the idea, he recognized its importance. Laura walked first to St. David's and continued from there along a rough path, toward Shipman's Corners. At Shipman's Corners, modern day St. Catharines, Laura had been told the only safe way was through the woods. The idea had been that the slippers and light clothing would convince questioners she was only going a short distance, but half way to Shipman's Corners, the slippers no longer protected her feet.

In the woods after Shipman's Corners, Laura walked for a time in the pines where needles made a soft and silent mat. The areas of pine, however, were limited and between pines and hardwoods, large tracts of thorns ripped her thin dress and her legs beneath. Blood dripped from her ankles. She began to worry if she could get there by nightfall.

Then the swamp appeared, green slime around
the edge, a snake stirred the water. After a pause
for courage, she drew a deep shuddering breath
and stepped in.

Clouds of mud welled up around her legs. She
had heard wolves earlier, one barked nearby.
She couldn't keep the tears away and the sharp
things in the swamp grabbed and stabbed and
poked. When she got to the river, the cool water
brought some relief but at the other side when
she tried to stand, every stone became a needle
of pain. She inched up the hill, the sounds of the
wolves still behind her.

When the gun was cocked and the two men who
were beside her yelled, "Woman!" "Woman!"
Laura was startled, then relieved she had found
the soldiers she had set out to warn.

When she could go no farther, a Caughnawaga
warrior picked her up and carried her to the
headquarters of Lieutenant James FitzGibbon
where her information was gratefully received.

Laura had covered over twenty miles from four in
the morning until early moonlight. The information
she brought made it possible for Lieutenant James
FitzGibbon to organize a defense that first surprised,
then completely routed the American Army. The
American Army outnumbered FitzGibbon's men,
nine to one but was completely confused by the
four hundred Caughnawaga warriors who shot
from moving cover. Fitzgibbon also added to the
confusion by marching his small force of uniformed
men here and there to make it look like he had a
force equal to the Americans.

The success of FitzGibbon and his men did not win
the war, but by standing firm in their important
defensive position, they shortened the war. Their
sucess convinced the American army that the
occupants of Canada would not give up without
a fight.

Jean McWilliam

In his speech to the Calgary *Next-of-Kin Association*, Richard Bedford Bennett said he had seen tears roll down the cheeks of Sir Robert Borden when the Prime Minister read the list of casualties from the war in France. In the question period that followed, Jean McWilliam asked him if he thought the Prime Minister had also cried when he saw the amount of allowance the soldiers' widows would get. Mr. Bennett was offended and demanded Jean appear before him the following day.

The next day, in his office, Bennett snarled, "Your inflammatory words are grounds for a charge of slander!" Jean snarled back, "The rest of the women in Calgary think you're God Almighty but you don't scare me a bit."

Jean's strength of conviction shut R.B. up and changed his attitude. Calgary watched as he championed her causes for the rest of his political career.

Jean McWilliam devoted her life to finding better treatment for neglected and underprivileged people.

Her neighbours would joke that she was "in trouble again" each time the police department's *Black Maria* arrived at her home to deliver a disadvantaged person into her care.

George Dixon

The fight had lasted seventy rounds.

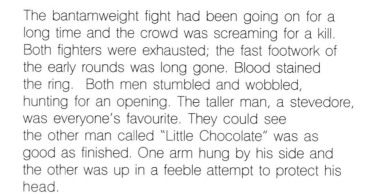

The bantamweight fight had been going on for a long time and the crowd was screaming for a kill. Both fighters were exhausted; the fast footwork of the early rounds was long gone. Blood stained the ring. Both men stumbled and wobbled, hunting for an opening. The taller man, a stevedore, was everyone's favourite. They could see the other man called "Little Chocolate" was as good as finished. One arm hung by his side and the other was up in a feeble attempt to protect his head.

The end of the fight was right in front of the stevedore. He raised his bloody knuckles to finish Little Chocolate when his weary eyes showed him something he couldn't understand. Little Chocolate was smiling. Little Chocolate was indeed very tired, but he'd put on the pretense of complete exhaustion to produce this critical moment when the stevedore would lower his guard. A flashing crack to the side of the stevedore's head put the man flat on the floor and silenced the crowd. George Dixon (Little Chocolate) won that bare-knuckle fight in the twentieth round. Five months before, the same two men had fought to a draw in a fight that had lasted seventy rounds.

Mr. Dixon was a champion, renowned for his courage and innovation. He is credited with the invention of the hanging punching bag and the practice of shadow boxing. He won 130 of his 158 professional fights and was the first fighter to hold both the bantamweight and the featherweight world titles at the same time.

George Dixon, was a photographer's apprentice from Africville, Nova Scotia, just around the corner from the Halifax garbage dump.

Nellie McLung

The "Premier" ended with the declaration that she was "unequivocally opposed to the enfranchisement of men in Manitoba."

The curtain opened in the Walker Theatre and the audience calmed its excited chatter. On the stage, a mock parliament was set with tables and chairs arranged in parallel rows. Women dressed in dark robes sat in the chairs. The first female speaker rose and spoke at length about the inappropriate nature of men's clothing. The second petitioned the government for labour-saving devices to help men. Members of the female opposition knitted, read newspapers and threw comments across the floor. "Yer just tryin to get in good with men."

The audience responded with ripples of laughter. A delegation of men stumbled across the floor of the mock house with a wheelbarrow full of petitions requesting the vote for men.

A man stood and respectfully made a plea for equal rights for men. When the petition ended, the *premier* (performed by Nellie McClung) rose to reply.

Nellie was a magnificent mimic and she had watched Premier Roblin the day before when he replied to a real petition presented to him by women.

Nellie hooked her thumbs in the armholes of her coat, twiddled her little fingers and teetered on her heels. She tucked her elbows into her waist, spread her hands to emphasize her reasonable position. Her voice was ingratiating and kind, it descended to graveled sincerity, suddenly switching to a loud commanding voice. The audience did not see Nellie; they saw their premier on the stage and they exploded into endless laughter.

They heard Premier Nellie explain that men could not have the vote. She "understood these misled men, they were downtrodden and disadvantaged but not all men were intelligent." "It is no use," she continued, "giving men the vote. They would misuse it – some voting too much - some voting not at all." How could men, "have the audacity to come asking for the vote when seven-eighths of court offenders were men?"

The audience was engulfed in laughter.

"Giving men the vote would unsettle the home."

"The modesty of our men, which we revere, forbids us to give them the vote - men may indeed be human but their place is on the farm."

By this time, the audience could not even hear Nellie because they were making so much noise themselves. The *Premier* ended with the declaration that she was, "unequivocally opposed to the enfranchisement of men in Manitoba."

When it was over, the applause and the laughter continued until the last members of the audience left the theatre.

The satire, concocted by a women's organization of which Nellie was a member, made enough money from the presentation to finance a move into the political arena and threaten Roblin's government.

Roblin resigned during a scandal a short time later.

Nellie McClung grew up in Manitoba and became a teacher and an accomplished author. She fought all of her life to improve the place of women in the Canadian Community. Her efforts were rewarded when women were recognized as "persons" under Canadian law in 1930.

Tsawwassa

It was a bad year for fires
and the old Chief was tired.

The Athapaskan and the surrounding tribes were competitive and aggressive. It was a bad year for fires and the old Chief was tired. He could feel it in his bones. He was not going to live forever. He planned well, the tribe pulled stakes and whisked away, down the mighty river.

They set up camp three nights later where the mountains fell away and the ocean washed the fringe of a richly endowed flat land. Here the river split into many courses and fish were abundant. The verdant soil fed wildlife of every variety and the people of his tribe were content.

Time passed; other tribes took a run at the new tenants but they had grown strong and they did not let their fighting skills lapse.

It was no surprise to all that Tsawwassa had equalled her brothers and returned as her brothers had with deer, bear, elk and fresh berries. At the end of her quest however, she had added shellfish from the ocean and and a bulb with flavour similar to an onion that grew on the ocean shore.

Today the beach where the onion still grows is called Tsawwassan Beach.

The old chief whose name was Tsatsen, showed his wisdom again when he decided his people needed a younger person to lead them. He instituted a contest between his two sons and his daughter in which he declared the hunter who brought the most food for the tribe in two days would become the new chief.

All agreed and set off indifferent directions. Two days later, his three children returned.

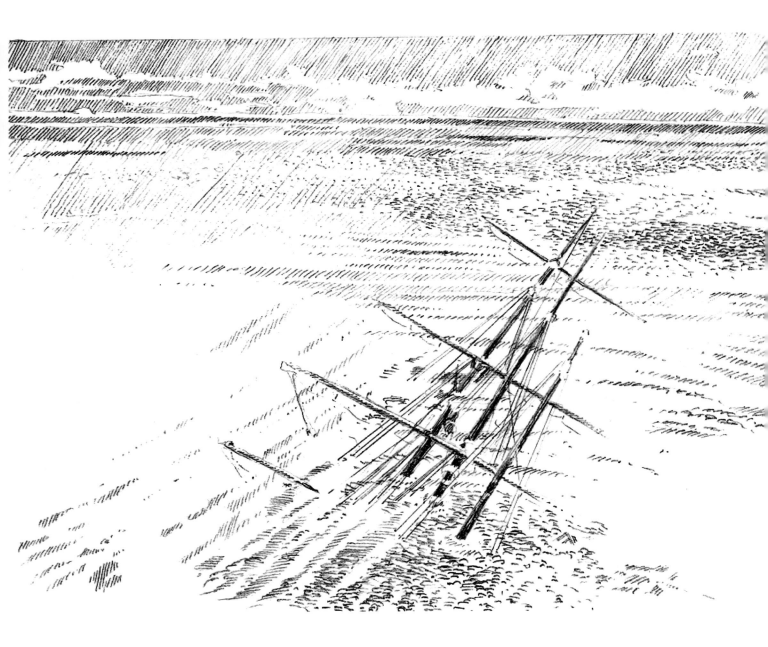

Mr. Dobbin

A partial list of ships sunk
along the Newfoundland coast
reads two hundred and fifty ships.

When a longboat with six survivors came ashore near the town of St. Lawrence in the first light of a Sunday morning, no one was surprised.

The townspeople leapt to their assistance, providing lodging and meals until transportation could be arranged back to wherever they had come from.

Those who came ashore included a captain, four crewmembers and a beautiful young blonde female passenger. The captain declared his ship the *Commaraskie* had hit a rock off Corbin's Head and these people were the only ones he was able to save. "Went down like a stone," he said. Soon the six were helped on their way and everything seemed to return to normal.

Then slowly, a feeling grew and the people of St. Lawrence began to greet each other with questioning looks. "Well?" said the man with arms like ham hocks to the skinny skipper across the fish table. "What'r'ya lookin' so ugly fer?" "Somethin' smells funny and it ain't my fish," said his friend in response.

A conversation between the two men opened the subject and soon others in the community added their thoughts. It was agreed. On close examination, the story of the survivors of the *Commaraskie* had "holes in 'er and was sinkin' fast." "There was a bit of a swell, but that storm was way out." "Ya can't get a longboat in the water through a disaster without puttin' a scratch or a scrape on 'er. That longboat was far and away too tidy…and why were they so calm?" "If they left a slew of passengers to die out there you'd think they'd be a bit upset." "Only the captain talked. Rest of 'em was all clammed up." "If only six could get away, how come they had time to pack their bags?"

The fishermen of St. Lawrence began an informal but well organized search for the sunken ship. They didn't interrupt their daily routines by much. They simply chose routes to their fishing grounds that would eventually cover all of the places the ship might have gone down. Word came back "no flotsam." Everyone asked the same question. "How can a ship with so many passengers hit a rock and sink without leaving a floating body or debris?"

The story was not fading; people became even more intrigued. There was a mystery here and they set out to solve it. Fishermen slowed their craft and began to look into the water rather than just scan the surface. Eventually off Corbin's Head, someone spotted a shadow on the bottom.

The call went out for Mr. Dobbin.

"Dobbin the Diver" was known along the eastern seaboard as the man most likely to solve a problem if that problem was below the surface of the water. Mr. Dobbin was also a person admired for his strength and courage. He arrived off Corbin's Head on a calm day with a boat and his equipment.

Diving equipment at that time included a canvas diving suit, lead shoes and a brass helmet resembling a large pumpkin with windows.

Hoses from the surface provided air. There was no communication between the diver on the bottom and the men above. Suited up, checked and rechecked, Dobbin was helped over the side and gradually lowered to the bottom.

Nothing he had experienced prepared him for what he saw next. The helmet didn't swivel, so he had to turn his body to face anything he wanted to see clearly. He caught a glimpse of something coming toward him and he turned to face it. A floating woman in a nightgown, arms outstretched, eyes wide, hands open and reaching, stunned him.

The floating woman brushed his shoulder then abruptly retreated. Three of her fingers snapped off as her hand bumped his helmet, two floated beyond him, one spun in place outside the right window of his helmet. He saw now the reason for her retreat. She was tethered to the mast by a rope tied to her waist - where Dobbin stood was the full length of her tether. Two men and another woman were tied on shorter restraints. All had floated here through days and nights for a month, performing their gentle three-dimensional dance. The two men whose ropes were tangled, embraced. One in nightwear and one without a shirt. Dobbin experienced a definite impulse to return to the surface to share his discovery. Instead, he slowly rotated on the spot to make sure of his surroundings and swallowing his fear, began to search.

In the windows of the locked doors of the lounge, three soft white faces and a bare leg pressed against the glass; high on the glass, a hand opened in exclamation.

He broke the lock and slowly pulled the doors outward. The bodies moved towards him as he created a new current with the doors. His terror now exchanged for sorrow, he sorted them and carefully pushed them upward towards the surface.

Inside the salon, sixty-three passengers waited patiently. Five were on the ceiling with the wooden furniture and articles from the tables. Some were tangled together and hung suspended, a few inches above the floor. One portly man sat in a chair on the wall. Everyone moved slowly in the current from the opened door. The movements of Mr. Dobbin created currents that made the body of a child seem to turn and follow him as he moved. As soon as he had released them to the men waiting above, he went looking for the crew.

Not surprisingly all thirteen men were found behind the locked doors that gave access to the ship below decks. Dobbin freed them, then took a cursory look through the ship to see if he had missed anyone. There were no more victims.

In the captain's cabin, the safe door swung slowly in the current, revealing an empty interior, very empty, very clean.

The bodies were taken and buried together at a place near Corbin's Head. The place of burial came to be known as the "Plantation." It was still visible as a green mound in the summer of 1915.

The captain and his team were arrested in England two years later. When confronted with the facts of his unbelievably cruel crime, he did not resist and provided the police with a full confession. At his hanging, he seemed relieved.

The four male accomplices received long sentences and the attractive young woman went free. She said she had feigned an attraction for the captain to escape the fate of the other passengers.

Dobbin continued his work and became the favourite subject of newspapers up and down the maritime coast. In the course of his career, he recovered over two thousand bodies and brought them to the surface for proper burial.

———

I searched obsessively for more information on this incredible story, sending messages to maritime museums and agencies asking for more information on what had happened to the Commaraskie. I thought if I was able to add a little more, perhaps the names of captain or crew, it would add to the story. In the end I found that one of the origins of the story was Memorial University of St. John's, Newfoundland and another, a series of articles in the Newfoundland Colonist in which Dobbin himself reflects on a ship he mistakenly identifies as the Commaraskie. A new book gives the correct description of the ship as a 600 ton barque named Monasco of Warren from the State of Maine carrying a cargo of iron from Sweden to the United States. The captain's name was Daly or Daily.

The date of the incident was July 21st, 1857 and the passengers were of Swedish origin. Also the captain wasn't hanged in England; he died by hanging after a trial in the United States.

Mathew Simser

Mathew's sixteen-month-old brother was active for his age. He pried the cover off a wall vent and went exploring. Well down the vent, the child got stuck and alerted everyone to his distress with loud wails. Mathew's mother located the child in the vents and Mathew found where to get into the vent system. Considering himself fearless, Mathew entered the vent head first.

It terrified him and he came back out twice. On his third try, he got far enough to grab a fistful of his brother's pants and pull him slowly backwards to the opening.

The 911 crew was knocking on the door as the sixteen-month-old was extracted from the vent.

Five-year-old Mathew was given a bravery award by the city of Toronto.
Mr. Simser screwed all the vents to the wall.

Angus Walters

For eight weeks, they'd caught,
cleaned and salted fish.
Now they were cargo fat,
happy and going home.

The bowsprit pointed its needle at the sky and brought it smashing down into a boiling sea. A cloud of sail, 10,000 square feet, billowed above and thundered against the straining ties.

The ship, a Grand Banks schooner from Nova Scotia with all its sails up and close-hauled for speed, seemed to be finely balanced on a tight steel line. Would it suddenly catch a corner and flip into the sea? A sharp northeasterly bellied the eight canvas sails and almost made it fly. Astern on the lee side, another schooner raced to pass the first. It was a joyful event that signaled a good catch.

For many years, fishermen who fished the Grand Banks raced for fun. The Halifax Herald decided to institute a contest to see who was the fastest working schooner in the North Atlantic. They offered the International Fishermen's Trophy to the ship that won a series of races off Halifax. An inflexible rule was the ships had to have fished on the Banks for at least one season.

Elimination races had to be held. Lunenburg alone had over one hundred schooners and there were hundreds more along the coast of Nova Scotia and the United States who wanted a shot at it. The race was set for October 11,1920.

A ship named the *Esperanto* won and took the Fishermen's Trophy home to Gloucester, Mass.

This was very hard on the proud Nova Scotians. They determined to find out why the American ship had won. In the end, they reasoned the American ship was faster because the American fish market was for fresh, not salted fish! The American ships stayed on the Banks for a much shorter time rushing smaller catches back to fresh fish markets. This made their ships lighter and faster.

The Canadians didn't want a fresh fish market but they did want a faster ship. Interested businessmen and sportsmen in Halifax got together and put the call out for a marine architect who could design a faster schooner. Canada didn't have a marine architect; new crafts were constructed from models, not plans.

William Roue's carved model won the contract for a faster schooner. The keel was laid at the Smith and Rhuland shipyards in Lunenburg late in the fall of 1920. She was launched on March 26, 1921 and handed over to the riggers.

In April 1921, the *Bluenose* headed out to the Banks for her first season of fishing.

From 1921 to 1931, every time the race was run, *Bluenose* took the International Fishermen's Trophy home to Nova Scotia.

Angus Walters of Lunenburg, an excellent captain on all points of sailing, was her captain through all of her races. His ability and the *Bluenose*, beat *Elsie*, *Henry Ford*, *Columbia*, *Haligonian*, and *Gertrude L. Thibaud* twice.

All the challenging ships were American.

Two-thirds of the way through the 1921 race against *Elsie*, *Elsie's* foretopmast broke. Captain Walters lowered his own foretopmast so his ship would not have an unusual advantage. The *Bluenose* still won the 40-mile race by twelve minutes.

Mrs. Copeland

The *Francis* went down off Sable Island and took nineteen passengers including the respected Dr. and Mrs. Copeland with it. The two were valued and popular members of Halifax society.

Two members of the rescue station team on Sable had seen the *Francis* trying to work her way free from a sandbar. The ship failed and during the night the surf smashed her into small pieces. Amongst the debris were trunks, papers, horses, a cow and Mrs. Copeland. The men's story was that when they went out in the morning, they found the pieces of the wreck and buried the late Mrs. Copeland.

A military officer was made aware that Mrs. Copeland was accustomed to wearing an unusually expensive ring. She had worn the ring for so long, it would not come off. The officer thought it over for a time and approached the men who had buried Mrs. Copeland. Knowing they were of a superstitious nature, he told them the following story:

He had gone to Sable for the grieving family to make sure of the burial. On his first night there, a woman had silently entered his camp and sat down beside him. Her long hair was dripping with water and her dress was covered with seaweed and sand. After staring at him for a time, she slowly placed her left hand on the sand in front of him to show the officer that her bloodied ring finger was missing. He explained to her that he understood her meaning and she faded away.

The terrified men, immediately confessed and produced the ring. The military officer informed the men they had avoided a serious penalty by confessing and returned the ring to an appreciative Copeland family.

Louise Arbour

Louise Arbour accepted the position of UN High Commissioner for Human Rights on February 20, 2004. Sergio Bieira de Mello, the man who preceded her, had been murdered.

Mme. Arbour was born in Montreal Quebec, where she attended a convent school and became editor of the school magazine. She graduated from the University of Montreal with a Bachelor of Arts degree. She became the Law Clerk for Mr. Justice Louis-Phillipe Pigeon of the Supreme Court of Canada while finishing graduate studies in law. In 1977, Ms. Arbour was admitted to the Ontario Bar.

Louise Arbour became a Research Officer for the Law Reform Commission of Canada and an Associate Professor and Associate Dean of Osgood Hall Law School. She was also Vice-President of the Canadian Civil Liberties Association until she was appointed to the Supreme Court of Ontario.

In 1996, Madam Justice Arbour was appointed Chief Prosecutor of War Crimes before the International Criminal Tribunal for Rwanda and the former Yugoslavia.

In 1999, Louise Arbour was appointed to the Supreme Court of Canada.

In 2006, Mme. Arbour strives to bind the wounds of the world working under the title of United Nations High Commissioner for Refugees.

Her work has added to and greased the engines of the world's justice systems.

Louise Arbour is amazing.

Arthur

One man's quiet wisdom.

Arthur's father was a less than tall Englishman who came west early, got a piece of land and homesteaded. When he arrived on the land not far from Red Deer Alberta, he had two dollars and a shovel. It was fall and he didn't have time to build a half n' half, so he dug a small cave in a sand hill, covered the door with canvas and lived there through the first winter.

Over time, this determined man built a home and a barn and a large ranch filled with about two thousand white-faced Hereford cattle. Arthur inherited the farm when he came of age, married a beautiful girl named Gwen, and soon babies appeared and the ranch grew and prospered.

A surrounding community had developed in support of the ranching families. There was a white Anglican church on the hill at the end of the valley. A schoolhouse was built over on the west side. There was a corner store at the top and everyone's home was open for meetings,

whether for a quilting bee, a tea and talk or meetings of select groups to settle community problems. The community worked well, hunger was non-existent and anger was an unusual event. Then as often happens when everything appears to be perfect, Arthur discovered a problem. The fabric of this perfect little community was at risk and only Arthur could keep it from falling apart. Gwen asked if he was all right. The minister of the church said he "seemed thoughtful." His children kept a careful distance.

Seven Irish brothers, wild and full of pranks, owned a ranch of similar proportions that ran along the east side of Arthur's property. The evidence was very clear; a section of wire had been cut and rigged so it could be reopened at will. Tracks told the story and twelve cows were missing.

In Canada, they didn't hang you for rustling but the jail term was long enough to hurt. Arthur assessed the damage done and the future damage possible. He pondered on what the news would do to the community and all the families on both sides of the issue; then he went back to being lost in thought, grumpy even.

One day his mood finally changed. He went to town and got thirty nickels. He took the nickels, sterilized them, got thirty cows, put a tiny cut in the shoulder of each and inserted a nickel. A strange investment. He took the cows down to the field where the other cows had been stolen, put them in place and waited. Soon twelve more cows had disappeared through the improvised gate in the fence. Royal Canadian Mounted Police patrols came around about twice a year so when the man in the Mountie uniform rode by on his horse, Arthur approached him. "Come for a ride with me? I have something I want to show you."

They rode over to the ranch of the seven brothers. On the way, Arthur explained to the constable what he had done.

The brothers gathered when they arrived. The constable asked them if they had any private way of identifying their cows. They said, "Just a brand and in fact this bunch here in the corral have just been gathered so we can brand them."

Recognizing some of the cows as his own, Arthur accused the seven brothers of stealing his cows. They just laughed and said they were certainly innocent and Arthur had certainly lost his mind. Arthur pointed to some of the cows around him and said, "Those nine are mine, and the three over there." "Prove it," growled a brother. So Arthur dismounted, went directly to two cows and slipped the nickels out of the slots in their shoulders. The seven brothers were caught. "Rustlers go to jail for a long time," Arthur said to the constable, "but if you will listen to my idea for a moment I may save you the time and expense of seven prisoners." On the constable's agreement, Arthur explained he did not want his neighbors to be charged. He simply wanted them to buy all of the cows in his herd. The brothers recognized this would mean a great deal of money. They also knew this solution was a lot better than jail. So the day ended with a confused constable and the seven brothers scrambling for money.

At the beginning of the following week, Arthur's two thousand, white-faced cows were transferred to the brothers' ranch through the new gate. Arthur was paid the full amount for healthy cows at the going rate.

On Tuesday, Arthur rode in to the Agricultural Fair Grounds in Red Deer and bought the first breeding stock he would need to build a prize winning herd of purebred (all black) Black Angus cattle.

No one but the eight men and the police constable knew what had taken place. No wives knew, no children were ever told and no cow ever again disappeared from Arthur's pasture.

This was Arthur's solution. The happy and prosperous valley would continue. The wives would continue to work together; the children would all still play together. Arthur's family and the seven brothers would keep the same adjacent pews in the church. The women would still pick Saskatoons, make their jam, quilt and hook rugs at the "Happy Hookers" club.

Arthur explained his reasoning to the constable on the ride back to his place. The constable ate dinner at Arthur's and rode away with a smile on his face.

Arthur seemed to smile a lot. Gwen still asked, "Are you all right?" But she really wasn't worried any more.

 Ghost Devil

Ghostpine Lake empties into Ghostpine Creek and Ghostpine Creek ambles southwards and joins hands with Three Hills Creek. The two creeks empty into the Red Deer River and the Red Deer carries the waters under the bridge and along beside the city streets of Drumheller. Ghostpine Lake and Ghostpine Creek were once Devil's Pine Lake because First Nations People, at the full moon, saw a ghostly "devil" always on the crest of a hill, always on a black horse. The locals called the lake Ghostpine and so it stayed until the postal service saw convenience as more important than history. Ghostpine became "Pine."

The legend of a ghost "devil" who rode the hills and the shores of the lake began before the whites arrived and grew from the true story of a group of First Nations People who decided to camp on a pleasant promontory on the eastern shore. In the night, an opposing band attacked the sleeping people and killed them all, men, women and children. What the attackers had no way of knowing was that a member of the slaughtered tribe was away hunting. He returned the next day to face the sight of his family members dead and mutilated.

Usually, vengeance amongst aboriginal people was swift and non-specific. If a member of a tribe was killed, acceptable justice was to kill any member of the killer's tribe in return. The lone survivor in our story didn't see it that way. He waited and planned, carefully learning the habits and movements of the tribe who had killed his family. Then one by one, at his convenience, he killed each of them. It is said his last victims died of terror without a mark on them. The vengeful rider had flowing black hair, was dressed in black rags, covered his face with charcoal and rode a fast black horse.

Upland game flourished. In the fall, ducks and geese declared this their "flyway." Blue-winged teal braked for the lake with the ripping sound of wings brought up to the wind at eighty miles per hour. Loons laughed. Children came to swim.

Soon the six a.m. to ten p.m. labours of the families produced enough wealth to build better homes.

In the winter, there were iceboats, skating parties and a lunatic with a model "A" who would get it up to fifty, turn the wheel and spin and spin all the way down the lake. One family moved a house across the lake when the ice was thick. It took three double teams and all the men of the community.

On cold mornings, lucky kids had an old plough-horse to ride to school, the oldest in front, down the line to the youngest. Occasionally they ended up without the youngest, when he or she slipped off the end. Five kids could get on Luke. Matthew, Mark and John had retired to pasture. The kids on the other side of the lake were rowed across when there was school and walked across on the ice in winter.

In 1913, the community hitched up its pants and donned the attitudes of war; everyone who could go, went. There wasn't a family that didn't make a contribution in tears and sorrow.

When the depression hit, living "in the country" was the best place to be. Each family had a few chickens, a cow, a pig and a vegetable garden, so they all survived. Golf-ball hail erased crops; half a son came home from war; someone put green hay in the barn and burned it down. People looked to each new day to solve yesterday's problem. Thinking was a good thing. Constant entertainment was not required. The Elliot boys found a wicker baby-buggy and smoked it down to the wheels.

People told their best lightning stories and were countered by someone with a better lightning story. Gregory's dad was racing home in a wagon to beat the storm. As he passed through the gate, a bolt hit the fence and zapped down the wire. It leapt the gate, removed his clothes and left him on the ground wondering what day it was. Nancy had St. Elmo's fire dance on her stove.

At full moon, when it repeats itself upside down in the lake, the residents look to see if there is a rider on a fast black horse on the crest of a hill near Ghost Pine Lake.

Otis Hyslar

Otis lived in Lunenburg. The town was renowned for its ability to build large wooden ships, like the *Bluenose* for racing and the *Bounty* for the famous movie, *Mutiny on the Bounty*. Otis was a seaman whose family had come from Holland to farm. Their ship floundered in a storm off Nova Scotia and when they came ashore they found perfect Lunenburg harbour. They stayed. Otis worked full time at any job that became available on anything that floated. He was of normal height vertically and almost the same horizontally. A French beret hugged his head and pure white stubble framed the tanned and wind-burned face. Huge forearms hung at his side with muscled fingers in hands twice the size of a normal man's. He lived alone in a tiny and impeccable white house on a short street that topped the town. The walkway to the front door was bordered in red, white and blue stones. Otis was happy to say that he had painted each one. Nothing inside was remarkable except for cleanliness and a living room wall filled with trophies. The largest trophy went away for a short time each year but always returned.

H.M.S. Bounty

The beautiful bodies of strong men and the rougher shapes of the more experienced, covered the pier on competition day. The dories were allotted and the men rowed their craft to the starting line. The gun went off and although the young men carried the first lap, the persistence of the older men pushed them ahead in later laps. Approaching the last lap, Otis, who was in the lead, slowed to give his competitors hope. A man in the crowd smiled. Everyone gave it their best but Otis crossed the finish line first by a length. While his exhausted competitors collapsed across their oars, Otis sat up straight, took the handles of his heavy twelve-foot oaken oars and turned them upwards with the strength of his forearms. The crowd knew his signature and filled the air with calls and cheers.

The man who smiled left the crowd to engrave the name `Otis Hyslar' on the cup once again.

Jung Mah

Jung Mah was the oldest of four children in a Chinese Canadian family. The family owned a restaurant on the main street of Madoc, Ontario. The children were expected to take a turn helping out in the restaurant. They all complied except for the youngest who had a few years to grow before his help would be required.

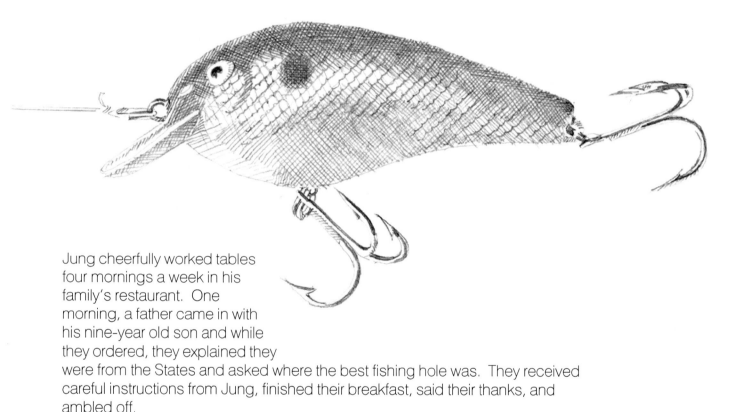

Jung cheerfully worked tables four mornings a week in his family's restaurant. One morning, a father came in with his nine-year old son and while they ordered, they explained they were from the States and asked where the best fishing hole was. They received careful instructions from Jung, finished their breakfast, said their thanks, and ambled off.

Later the same day, the father turned up at the local hospital carefully clutching his son's hand that had a fish hook well embedded in its thumb. The father was made comfortable by a reassuring nurse and was doing fine until the doctor who showed up to remove the hook was the same man who had served him breakfast.

Jung Mah was a family physician with hospital privileges. He continued his education and became Clinical Professor of Orthopaedic Surgery at McMaster University in Hamilton, Ontario.

Robert Rundle

'Hmmmph!' said the bull buffalo,
It's only a missionary."

On a walk outside Fort Edmonton, Robert Rundle was startled by a group of sled dogs who gave him a clear indication they would like to have him for dinner. The following day, he joined a group of men hunting buffalo. As they raced behind the herd, a large bull glanced over its shoulder and seemed to say, "Hmmph! It's only a missionary." The bull turned and charged Rundle, knocking both the minister of the gospel and his horse to the ground. While the animal decided which way to sit on the Reverend, his companions caught up with the drama and chased the bull away.

Before Reverend Rundle said goodbye to a group of Cree, he hid his cat in his bags for safety and tied a string to its leg just in case it got away. Aboriginal people knew of cats only in their larger sizes such as lynx and cougar. The tiny version in the Reverend's bag was not within their range of experience.

When the cat, at the least appropriate moment, was accidentally flipped into the air by a tug on its string, the Cree were astonished. The cat reached the full extent of the string and snapped back, landing on the horse's leg with all claws extended.

The horse took it personally, dumped Rundle and his bags on the ground and took off across the prairie.

Sitting in the mud with a cat on a string, the Reverend Rundle did not look like a man who had influence with the Almighty.

It took the Cree, who had come to say goodbye, a long time to recover from their fits of laughter. As they travelled east towards their home, the group would regain its composure for a time, then suddenly at a sound or gesture, dissolve again into endless laughter.

In spite of his unreliable relationships with animals, Reverend Rundle made a respectable contribution to the growth of communities in the early west.

The southern backdrop for the beautiful town of Banff, Alberta is a large mountain named Rundle, named for the missionary and his early work.

Lumber Jacks

Two Jacks, Jack from Ontario and Jacques from Quebec, stole a small boat from the Vancouver docks and rowed north along the coast of British Columbia. Looking for work, they checked the lumber camps as they went and finally, just past the one hundred mile mark, they found jobs,

Neither of the young men had worked in a lumber camp before and at first they heard many words they didn't understand. Every time they were given something to do, they had to ask what the "something" was. Jacques was sent for a *Molly Hogan*. One man said it was a measuring device, another said it was a 'keeper'. The *Molly Hogan* request was a joke similar to the request for a *board stretcher* that novice carpenters are sent to fetch.

In the dark of early morning after a robust breakfast, the two men were introduced to a *crummy*. The *crummy* was Transportation Central's battered bus. It took them past a sign that read, " 0-DAYS WITHOUT ACCIDENT" to a loading site called a *trackside*. The fallen trees were *bucked* (cut to length). The loaded logs were huge, often just one per eighteen-wheeler. The flexible steel cable that encircled each log was a *choker*; its sliding lock was a *bell*. The smaller steel cable that pulled the choker back into the bush was a *haulback*. A pile of logs not at trackside, was a *colddeck*. The man who blew the whistle to control the cables was called a *whistlepunk*. The electronic whistle was blown three times for stop, twice for go, ten whistles was a call for medical help, thirteen… a death. Nails on the bottom of boots for walking on fallen trees were called *corks*. Work stopped when snow filled the *corks* because slipping from the top of three criss-crossed trees was the same as falling from a three story building. The men couldn't trust the ground under the fallen trees. Rivers and streams could be heard beneath the brush that fallen trees had crushed. The pulleys in the semicircle of catchment were called *blocks*. The farthest block was a sixty pound *tailblock*. Carrying the *tailblock* through tangled and downed trees was the worst job in camp.

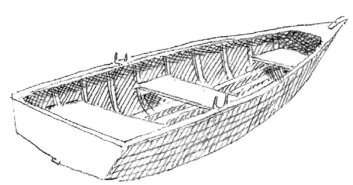

The two Jacks decided that in bad times, an acceptable wage and good food out-weighed both the dangers of the camp and rowing back south, one hundred miles.

Miiki & Morita

They did a little dance and
everyone yelled, "We won! We won!"

The mountains to the west jammed their steel points above the tree line showing patterns of white left over from winter. Snow released itself to cool mists and the first light of morning changed mountain shoulders to brown bread and butter. The mists slipped free, parting and joining then flowing like water in the folds of the mountain. Cold heights gifted the valley floor with cool breath and sharp diamonds on gilded spikes of rich green grass.

A Union Jack fluttered in Mrs. Morita's little garden. The sound of the aging Ford two-ton brought most awake.

The tarpaper buildings puffed out the first efforts of paper and kindling to warm the inhabitants' stoves. Doors opened and people went to the stream for water. A man stood in the road. He yawned and stretched his thick body, then quietly settled, Buddha-like, on the fringe of the road.

Mothers cared for babies. Children prepared for school in the house up the road. The two-family dwellings exuded heat waves from hot metal chimneys. Half-opened windows oozed the pleasing hum of morning chatter. Teachers readied to teach. Men gathered where roads crossed. It was a normal day.

Suddenly, Mr. Miiki's kid came flying down the road with a newspaper held high in both hands, the headlines for all to see. He yelled to all the faces that appeared in doors and windows, "We won! We won!" As he advanced down the road, other young people rushed to join him, "We won! We won!" they called. He did a little dance and everyone laughed. "We won!"

The place where they were living had been a mining town. The Canadian Government had filled the old hotel, a bunkhouse and a log cabin with families, then brought in a bulldozer and flattened the ground. On the raw stones, they built two long rows of tarpaper sheds. Each shed now contained two families.

The families were Canadian citizens of Japanese heritage who had been taken without just cause from their homes on the British Columbia coast and moved to valleys in the interior. The first to be removed were fishermen and the men and families who built fishing boats. Their licenses to fish, boats for work and boats for pleasure were taken from them.

The Canadian Government sold their belongings to strangers. Homes, cars, possessions and the ability to earn a living were taken from them. They were moved away from the ocean to camps with names like Sandon, Tashme, Kaslo, Greenwood, Slocan, Bayfarm, Popoff, Lemon Creek and New Denver. Families were often permanently broken. The elderly were separated from their younger families. The internments were so sudden and unexpected, many never saw their family members again.

Everything was taken. No financial compensation was offered or given. And no properties were ever returned.

No act of espionage and no accusation of espionage was ever brought against a Canadian of Japanese heritage during or after the Second World War.

Sadakichi Shichi was the first Japanese-Canadian to die in the First World War. 54 other men of Japanese origin died in that war and 93 were wounded.

Lefty

He was as smooth and graceful as a dancer.

Lefty was a cowboy; he knew horses nose to tail and inside out. To him, a horse's leg was a cannon bone and a fetlock with a frog on the bottom. Novice riders loved to watch Lefty throw a lasso. He was smooth and swift, as graceful as a dancer. It was "all in the wrist" he would say whether he flipped it underhand for a leg or looped one over for the farthest neck.

On a thirty-mile ride from Crimson Lake Alberta, twelve riders were chaperoned by Lefty to ensure their safety. About two-thirds of the way along, they passed a farm that had seen better days. In the yard, a boy of twelve stood in front of a leggy colt that was covered in sores. One leg was shorter than the others. Three legs splayed out in a tripod attempt to hold up the feeble body. The boy held a .22 rifle. Tears poured down his face and dripped from his chin. The colt had three small bullet holes perfectly centered between its watery eyes. Lefty dismounted quickly and went over to the boy who began to sob helplessly. He told Lefty the colt was not well enough to live and he had been trying to put it out of its misery. Lefty spoke to him quietly, then took the gun and dispatched the colt with a single shot. The brain, Lefty explained, was up between the horse's ears and not between his eyes.

The boy sat beside the dead colt until the riders were out of sight. A subdued ride made camp that night in an old logging camp.

Two days later, a call came in from a rancher in Water Valley. The man wondered if Lefty would come and get a wild horse he had captured but couldn't tame. Lefty had always said there wasn't a horse on earth that wouldn't respond to patience and caring. He chose Rick to go with him to help load the horse. Rick seemed a strange choice. He was not a graceful rider, did not sit well on a horse and was almost as wide as he was tall. His nickname was "Brick."

On the way to Water Valley in the old Ford, Lefty told Rick he had chosen him for his strength and because he was not afraid to get dirty. Rick glowed. He had never been singled out for anything but barbs and smart remarks. He determined then and there to be a useful partner for Lefty. The rancher had never seen a horse quite like this one before. He had to add three more rails to his corral just to contain the animal. The big black was very aggressive and liked to climb.

Lefty backed into a ditch and touched the box to a grassy embankment so they wouldn't have to use a ramp. The horse was indeed aggressive. Lefty put a loop on the horse then put a half hitch over his nose. Eventually, it took two ropes and two half hitches over its nose before Rick and Lefty could move it an inch. The two ropes were handy because the black would flatten his ears and take a run at Rick. Lefty held the horse away from Rick and when the horse would take a run at Lefty, sturdy Rick would hold him away from Lefty. They worked it so that the charging horse charged more in the direction of the truck than away from it and in that way they got him to the back of the truck. This black was smart. He saw three walls and he was not going into that trap. Lefty ran his rope through a ring in the front wall of the box and tried to pull the horse forward. The horse obliged. He raced onto the truck, leapt the front wall and ended up on top of the cab and engine. Flailing hooves turned the truck into a dented wreck. Twice more he went over the box walls. Lefty attached additional stock racks to extend the height of the truck walls. The black punched holes in the slats and went over the sides onto the ground. After five hours of struggles, something changed and the black seemed to ask, "Oh, you just want me to get in this box and stand there?" He climbed into the truck and stood there. Lefty secured him to the front of the truck box and Rick closed up the rear gate. A gentle rain had turned into a steady downfall as the truck pulled out of the ditch onto the road. Water Valley roads were surfaced with clay and the track soon became very slippery. There was a hill. The truck struggled to reach the top but couldn't on the first try. On the second try, they were all set to proclaim success when there was a mighty crash and a hoof smashed through the back window of the cab. Lefty yanked the emergency on. The truck was still sliding when he was out of the cab, over the racks and into the box where his feet flew from under him and he crashed down beside the black. The two lay side by side until Lefty recovered. Both had slipped on greasy clay that coated the floor.

The Black's feet had gone out from under him and while thrashing around to regain his feet, he hit the wall of the truck with that vulnerable spot between his ears that held his fragile brain.

Albert Mervin

He didn' have much to say.

Soldiers of the Soil.

In 1916, with many of the prairie men away from their farms fighting the First World War, children were allowed to stay away from school to work the fields. The children were much appreciated and earned the title *Soldiers of the Soil*.

Albert was twelve and his sister Luella was thirteen. They hitched the family team to a wagon filled with provisions, tied a plough, a harrow, a mower and a hay rake in line behind, and set out to travel to work on a quarter-section of land. Once the travellers were on the road, they could just make out a tiny dot eighteen miles ahead. The tiny dot was the only tree on the landscape and it sat on the edge of the property they were going to work.

Many years later, this very flat land would become the Edmonton Airport.

Albert and Luella spent two years working from early spring until first frost. When the war ended, they returned to school without the knowledge the other students had gained. *Soldiers of the soil* were many school lessons behind. Luella did well, Albert stumbled. An out-of-sorts teacher, instead of recognizing his own failure, snapped, "Why are you so stupid?" Albert stood up, left the school and never returned.

Not long after, their house near Leduc burned to the ground.

They found a house to rent not far away and Albert's father did his best to grow horseradish. His mother made meals for traveling families, while Albert walked the fringes of farmers' fields with a shotgun. He regularly brought home prairie chicken, partridge or a rabbit for dinner. They lived under a waterfowl flyway and in the fall when an evening sky was filled with ducks, Albert would bring home a smile and a Mallard drake or three.

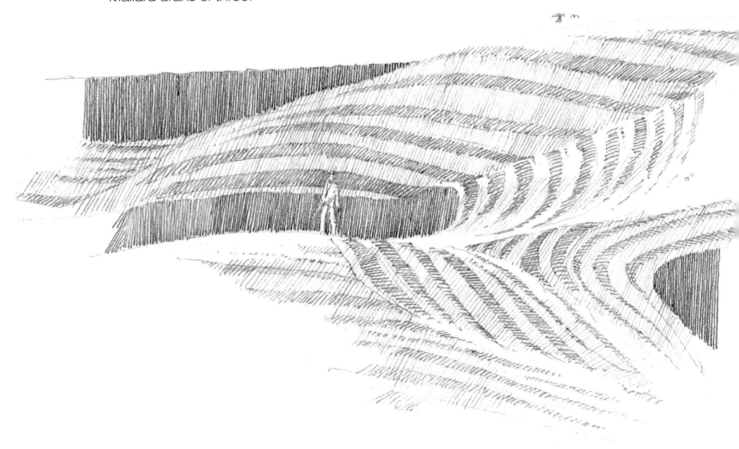

The sad part of this story is that for the rest of his life, Albert defended himself against the word that hurt so much, by choosing to speak little and if he had to, carefully. He taught himself what he wanted to learn and worked out a way for his interest in numbers to grow into an occupation where he did not have to talk very much.

A student at the Provincial Institute of Technology and Art in Calgary handed in his assignment three days late. He understood a penalty of five percent per day would be applied for his tardiness. The assignment was returned to him with one hundred percent marked in bright red pen on each of the drawings.

Feeling guilty for stealing the extra marks, the student asked Dr. Kerr if he would like to adjust the mark downward to accommodate the five percent per day penalty. Dr. Illingworth Kerr replied quietly and firmly. "I am the president of this school and if I want to mark your assignment at one hundred percent, I get to do that."

The doubt that every young artist hides inside himself was erased.

Illingworth Kerr

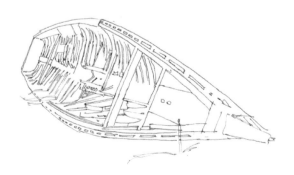

Daniel McGinnis

He knew there was pirate treasure
somewhere among the islands of Nova Scotia.

On a summer day in 1795, Daniel McGinnis and his two friends John and Anthony, began to dig.

Within the first two feet, they discovered a flagstone floor. They dug below the flagstones through loose dirt with a hard clay perimeter, for ten feet. At the ten-foot level, they found a platform of four-inch oak beams with their ends firmly set in the clay perimeter. They dug on and at twenty feet, a second and identical platform appeared and at thirty feet, a third. At the end of three days of exhausting labour, the sum of their discovery was a thirty-two foot clay tube with carefully constructed and identical platforms at ten-foot intervals.

Young Daniel had heard about pirates and privateers hiding among the islands of Mahone Bay, Nova Scotia. As early as he could remember, he was told that when a pirate collected enough booty, he selected an island, dug a hole and buried his treasure. If a pirate had ever made a deposit on one of Mahone Bay's hundreds of islands, Daniel McGinnis was going to be the one to find it.

Each summer he and his friends roamed about, sniffing and scratching and finding nothing. Then one day, alone on tiny Oak Island, Daniel stepped into a clearing and froze in front of a thirteen-foot wide, two-foot deep, depression in the ground.

For some reason, the three young men took a rest until 1802, when they reappeared with Simon Lynds. Mr. Lynds and the young men had formed a company called the Onslow Company to give their treasure hunting a better financial base. The tube-like shaft had fallen in but they dug it out and proceeded downwards to the ninety-foot level. Each of the new oak platforms, again at ten-foot intervals was now covered with a fibrous matting, charcoal and putty. Sitting on the ninety-foot platform with an indecipherable message cut into it, was a large flat stone. They retired for the night in a state of high excitement. When they returned in the morning, the tube they had worked so hard to empty, was full of water. Pumping turned out to have no effect on the level of the water.

The following spring, Onslow Company dug a shaft one hundred and ten feet deep beside the treasure shaft. Shaft number two filled with water to exactly the same depth as the treasure shaft. In 1849, the Truro Company used augers to drill below the platform with the rock on it. They drilled through the ninety-foot platform that turned out to be made of five-inch spruce.

After the spruce, the auger fell through empty space for twelve inches, then drilled four inches through oak, twenty-two inches of random metal pieces in which there were three links of a fine gold chain. Then came eight inches of oak, twenty-two inches of more loose metal, four inches of oak and six inches of spruce. Below the spruce was seven feet of clay.

The following year the Truro Company tried again, this time with a shaft (number three). It filled with water as soon as they got to the bottom and tried to access the treasure shaft. Two pumps operating day and night for two weeks could not lower the water an inch.

Critical information was gleaned by Truro in its second try. The water in the shafts was salt and it rose and fell with the ocean tides. Examination of a small cove north of the shafts produced three eight-inch holes where the ocean flowed into the ground.

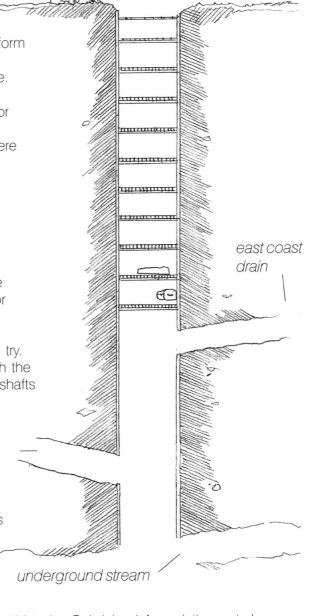

east coast drain

drain to the south shore —

underground stream

Each of these drains was surrounded by tons of fiber matting identical to the matting found on the platforms of the treasure shaft. Below the matting, beach stones were arranged in a distinctive pattern. Truro constructed a dam across the mouth of the cove and lowered the water level to investigate further. They found two more drains and a master drain fed by the smaller ones. From the master drain, they assumed a flood tunnel ran to the treasure shaft. So they dug down between the cove and the shafts, found the flood tunnel and blocked the flow of water. Ha! This was it, all they had to do was pump the shafts dry and the treasure would be found.

Wrong. Their best pumping efforts lowered the water only six inches. Truro Company was out of money and knowing they were fiddling with a booby trap that protected something, they were forced to end their hunt.

In 1861, the Oak Island Association put down shafts seven and eight. In shaft eight, the bottom became clogged with mud, the pit produced a roaring sound and more mud filled the bottom. Suddenly there was a second roar, all the mud went away and the bottom dropped five feet. Shafts nine, ten and eleven were dug to no avail and the Oak Island Association was out of money.

In 1878, a young woman plowing a nearby field was suddenly plopped with her oxen into a ten foot hole. The ground collapsed beneath her.

A message carved in stone and
found at the ninety-foot level looked like this.

In1893, the Oak Island Treasure Company dug shafts twelve and thirteen. When they failed with the shafts, they drilled a series of holes along the line of the flood tunnel, filled them with dynamite and blew up the flood tunnel. Seawater continued to flood the treasure shaft. Mr. Blair, who owned the Oak Island Treasure Company chose to resort again to augers to drill for information. He drilled through clay, cement and wood and at one hundred and seventy one feet bumped into solid iron. On checking the drill residue, a small piece of parchment was found.

Seven more shafts were dug - all of which were abandoned. The single real piece of information Mr. Blair brought to the search was the discovery of a second flood tunnel that brought seawater from the south shore of the island to the treasure shaft. The Oak Island Treasure Company ran out of funds.

In 1967, a company named Triton drilled holes around the spot they guessed the treasure shaft had been. At depths below where anyone had gone before, they found bits of oak carbon dated to 1575 - two hundred and twenty years before Daniel, John and Anthony had begun their dig.

A geological study of Oak Island reveals the island to be markedly different from the rest of the Atlantic coast of Nova Scotia. Instead of the usual hard granite underlying glacial deposits, Oak Island is underlain by anhydrite, a material resembling putty, full of pockets of limestone and salt.

In 1969, Triton Alliance began an intense, professional, twenty-year study of the site. They used augers, drills, cameras and sonar devices. They discovered an extensive network of man-made tunnels in the material beneath the treasure shaft. From an underwater camera, looking out of a drill hole into a cavern (at an undisclosed depth), they saw a hand, three chests and a human form lying against a wall.

In 1909, Henry Bodoin dug enough shafts to completely destroy the landscape and for a time no one knew where the first shaft had been.

In 1931, William Chappell dug shaft number twenty-one and found old tools at one hundred and sixty-three feet.

In 1959, Bob Renstall went to check shaft number twenty-seven. He fell in and drowned, along with his son and two other men who attempted to rescue him.

In 1936, Mr. Gilbert Hedden discovered an ancient skidway in the north cove and a triangle of stones that resembled a sextant and two surface boulders, with one careful hole drilled in each.

A causway made in 1575 closed off the cove so the water could be drained and construction of the drains and tunnel could take place.

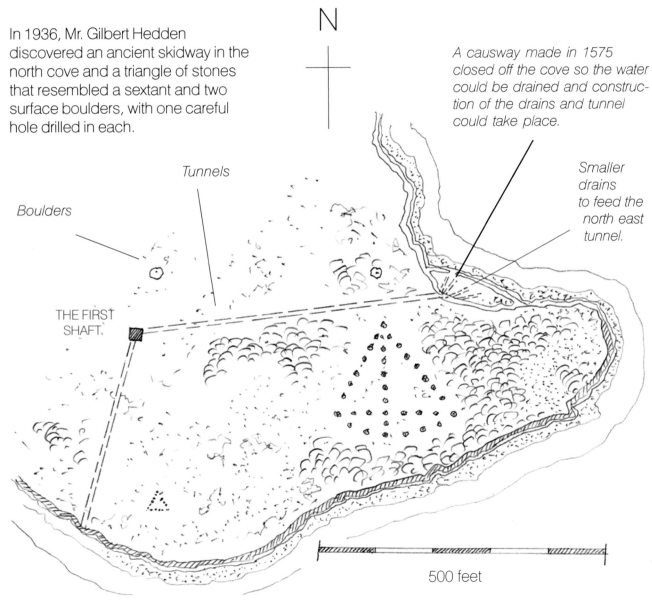

N

Smaller drains to feed the north east tunnel.

Tunnels

Boulders

THE FIRST SHAFT.

500 feet

The Island has been purchased by a private individual who does not dispense news of further attempts to find the treasure.

Lester Pearson

Lester B. Pearson was the Canadian Governments Minister for Foreign Affairs in 1956. He conceived and presented an idea to the United Nations Security Council for resolving territorial conflicts. The U.N. adopted his idea. Since that time, the world has watched as soldiers from many countries, dressed in the U.N. uniform work to keep warring factions apart. Often their efforts are successful. Occasionally they are not.

Mr. Pearson was awarded the Nobel Peace Prize in 1957 for his work in resolving the Suez Canal Crisis. He became Canada's fourteenth Prime Minister and responsible for instituting the search for a unique Canadian Flag.

In June 1993, the U.N. asked Canada for a high-ranking military officer to command a peacekeeping mission in the country of Rwanda. Canada gave them General Romeo Dallaire. Rwanda sits in the middle of the lake region of east-central Africa. The lakes that surround it feed the streams and rivers that flow into the mighty Nile. Historically, there have been two ethnic structures in Rwanda, the Hutu and the Tutsi. The Hutu had pushed a large part of a Tutsi minority out of Rwanda and into camps to the north. In three years, the Tutsi

refugees had constructed an army named the Rwandese Patriotic Front and attacked south-ward on foot and bicycle to regain the place they considered home. The majority Hutu population of Rwanda had a motorized army that was supported by French military and was called the Rwandese Government Forces. The RGF rushed north to stop the southward thrust of the RPF.

It was these two armies General Dallaire was asked to keep apart. Hidden from Dallaire was the reality of the blind hatred of the Hutu that incited them to organize militia units to secretly murder all of the Tutsi and moderate Hutu left in Rwanda. The disciplined and brilliantly led RPF continued to advance southward step-by-step, calmly waiting between each step to organize well for the next advance.

The Hutu extremists felt time was limited and rushed to do their killing…100,000 dead became 300,000 that became 500,000 dead men, women and children.

Romeo Dallaire

The RPF approached the capital, step by careful step. The militia gangs of the RGF moved to rural areas and killed and killed. A pontoon bridge over a river tilted with the weight of bodies pressing against it. A pile of dead at the hospital reached twenty feet in height. Roads and ditches filled. The smell of death covered the country wall to wall and a thousand feet thick…800,000 dead.

At General Dallaire's headquarters, as the killings became known and as the RPF continued to step southward, General Dallaire asked the U.N. for a force large enough and a mandate broad enough, to stop the burgeoning genocide. He was promised and then refused. He was given approval and had it yanked away. He was promised troops who never arrived. When it was imperative that he move, he was held in place. To save lives, he needed to move offensively and was told that he must not fire unless fired upon. The dead piled up in Rwanda. The rivers filled with mutilated corpses. And the U.N. was crippled by the self-interest of its member nations. The United States, France and Belgium looked only to their own interests and ignored the needs of dying Rwandans. Supplies froze. Dallaire's HQ was continually undersupplied. They worked without wavering and slept in their clothes. Mortar shells rained down. Dallaire rushed from participant to participant with persuasion as his only weapon. He worked on the fringe of exhaustion, unable to get the U.N. to act. Hutu hate-radio put out the message, "Kill Dallaire." He began to look upon the deaths of the innocents as the product of his inability to get the United Nations to do its job.

Late to the story, the press arrived. The world became a witness and the member states of the U.N. were shamed into action. The peace-keepers began to get food. Water for bathing was no longer rationed to a single cup a day. Staff who were showing signs of mental exhaustion were given a short break. Dallaire's mental condition began to slip and instead of resting, he worked, now intentionally taking the dangerous routes as he rushed here to help and there to convince.

As the RPF brought the situation to an end by winning the war and putting a democratic government in place to run the country, the U.S. and France stepped into the bright lights of the press cameras and managed to be seen as bringing aid to Hutu refugees. The aid, instead of helping them return to their reconstructed country, locked the Hutus in place in camps along the borders of Rwanda. They began to build yet another army.

The United Nations failed Rwanda. General Dallaire did not.

Bob Bartlett

The game was who could get across
the harbour fastest by leaping
from ice pan to ice pan.

Bob Bartlett was the son of a Newfoundland captain who was the son of a Newfoundland captain who was the son of a captain. Bob was raised in Brigus, Newfoundland. He was born of brine and ancient stone shores and as he grew and collected the parts and pieces of a New-foundland upbringing, he fostered an affection for music, ice of all kinds and ships of all shapes.

In winter, Brigus harbour was filled with ships waiting for spring. There were so many ships, the townsfolk could walk across the harbour on their decks. The children loved to play on the ice; their favourite game was a foot race across the harbour on the moving pans of ice. There was no certain route from one side to the other and the condition of the ice could change daily with wind and weather. Exuberant competitors leapt onto pans, raced as fast as they could to the next available pan before the one they were on tipped or sank. Pan to pan, they raced from one side of the harbour to the other. If pans of the right size were in the right place, they made it to the other side, winded but dry. Those who did not judge the ice well, ended up in very cold water. One day Bob went home soaked for the seventh time to find he was out of clothes. He borrowed a dress from his sister and rushed back to win the next race. Bob's love and knowledge of ice was the found-ation for his eventual reputation as the greatest ice captain in the world. Ocean ice was his toy. As he matured, his love of ships was clear and at the age of sixteen, he was running schooners for his father and his uncles. At twenty-one, he went to sea in four-masted freighters to earn his master's papers. Bob's mother wanted him to enter the Methodist ministry but Bob wanted to sail the frozen oceans of the north and listen to music on his gramophone.

In the sunless days of the winter of 1914, a ship captained by Bob, was caught by pack ice west of Herschel Island and pulled west and north to a position two hundred and fifty miles above the coast of Siberia. The ship was slowly compressed by the ice. Beams cracked, the deck bowed outwards until the ship burst and sank, slipping out of sight beneath the ice, and leaving twenty-two men, one woman and two children standing in the wind on the arctic ice.

Bob's advice to his passengers was to follow him and walk to an island so the moving ice would not take them out of reach of rescue. The four men who chose to ignore Bob's advice died on the ice. Bob left the surviving group on the island, then he and an Inuit hunter named Katak-tovick walked six hundred miles to find a rescue ship. The fourteen people who listened to Bob's advice lived. One man lost his mind.

An experienced ice captain can look at the ice flowng past his ship and know where the ice comes from, what it means, where it is going. A captain of Bartlett's experience knew why the moving pile of ice on the horizon was dangerous and why ice suddenly came apart and a river of flowing water appeared without reason. Captain Bob knew the language of the ice; ice had a personality; it sang and it hummed. It moaned, groaned, growled, exploded and spit. It tested a man's sanity with long stretches of absolute silence. The sun goes around and around in the summer without setting. It blazes down without heat, then blazes back up from the ice. The light can take a man's sight if he is unwary. Ice ridges and ice rafts. Rafting happens when the wind on the open ocean gets up and pushes the ice hard enough to make it climb onto itself and slide along the top surface. Rafted ice often comes in multiple layers and travels fifty miles wide, at the speed of the wind. If the wind is strong, it pushes racing walls of ice that erase everything in their path.

Rafted ice that had accumulated in enough layers to be twice as tall as the ship's deck, pushed one of Captain Bob's ships up onto the land and left it high and dry, lying on its side. Bob froze a post into the moving ice, tied a sturdy rope and let the moving ice pull his ship off the land. Ocean ice often makes "growlers." Growlers are small icebergs that travel with floe ice. They can catch any ship unaware and make it vulnerable. A growler can suddenly split, creating two icebergs that tumble and make a big enough wave to tip a ship. Captain Bob was known as the man who best spoke the language of the northern ice.

It was no surprise when he was chosen by the American explorer Robert Peary to be his guide and ship's captain on Peary's attempt to be first to reach the North Pole. Bob Bartlett's job was to put Peary at the top of Ellesmere Island and then, because he was experienced in surviving the north, prepare a safe path for Peary over the ice to the Pole.

Captain Bob hired a crew of Newfoundlanders for the American ship that was built for Peary's attempt. When they eventually sailed for the Pole, there were only two Americans on board, Peary and his manservant, Mr. Henson. With great effort, Bob took

Peary through the ice to the top of the North American land mass and then prepared a safe path northwards on the ice to a spot, one hundred and fifty miles from the Pole.

Peary had promised Captain Bob that he could accompany him on this last leg. Peary reneged on his promise. Peary and his manservant went alone.

Albert Failles

Albert Failles decided he was too old
to trap in the minus sixty-degree temperatures of
northern winters. Instead, each succeeding winter
he prepared for a spring departure on his personal
project. When the ice left the river, Albert packed
supplies for two months and headed out.

The search was not for gold or riches; he didn't
need riches. Albert just wanted to solve two
problems that had bothered him for a long time.
Where were the legendary McLeod brothers
and where was their claim?

The first leg of the trip took him southwest, up the
Liard River from Fort Simpson for one hundred
miles. At that point, he swung right or northwest
into the land of the Naha where the South Nahanni
pours into the Liard. He then continued up the
South Nahanni into Deadman's Valley. Martin
Jorgensen and Angus Hall were found here without
their heads. Along a bit, Chevac and Homburg
starved to death. Bill Eplar and Joe Mullholland
just disappeared. May Lafferty walked away in a
straight line to nowhere, taking her clothes off
piece by piece as she went. No one found her,
just her clothes. Hell's Gate is here, where white
water challenges any craft. Canyon One is
by Canyon Two and the vertical self-importance
of the Pulpit.

After one hundred more miles up the South
Nahanni, Albert would arrive at the bottom of

Virginia Falls. The Falls from the bottom were very
impressive and it looked like a long way to the top.
It was. Virginia Falls at twice the height of Niagara
Falls, is a 2,500-foot climb. He couldn't go through
it, so he had to climb around it.

As he had done on each of his previous trips,
Albert pulled his scow onto the shore below the
falls and carefully unloaded. He placed his
supplies in tidy piles, each pile representing how
much he could carry in a single trip to the top.
There were several piles for groceries, two for tools,
three metal drums of gasoline at one drum per trip,
the outboard motor and finally what appeared to
be a last pile for odds and ends. After the many
hours of up and down the trail, Albert crouched
and placed his back against a canvas sack that
held the motor. He placed straps over his shoulders
and leaned forward, away from the load. It was too
heavy for him to tilt onto his back. He reached
forward and picked up a stone. The weight of the
stone tipped him forward and the load was then in
a position for him to lift and carry. The motor was
not to be his last load. He returned to the base of
the falls and pulled out eight long boards he had
stored in the bottom of the scow. The boards were
twelve feet long, fourteen inches wide and one
inch thick. Each board became one more trip to
the top. When he came down for the last board,
he pulled the now empty scow as far up the bank
as he could and tied it firmly to a rock. The scow
represented his escape in the fall.

Now, over three days, he would build a second
scow from the boards he had pulled to the top of
the falls. He cut the lengths with a swede saw and
the shapes with an axe. Caulking cracks and
gumming holes each took a day. Then, after he
was finished and content with his labours, he had
a good sleep, a good breakfast and packed up
to continue up the river.

Albert never told anyone exactly where he was
going. Someone had seen him once, a hundred
miles above the falls near Headless Creek where
the Flat River and the South Nahanni come
together. He always went alone and never filed a
flight plan.

Above Virginia Falls, the Nahanni becomes a
wide and meandering river that alternates from

deep and fast to very wide and very shallow. In the shallow places, rippling water gathers volume and speed for the dramatic plunge down the falls.

Now, in a shallow place and well out in the middle of the river, Albert stands with his newly constructed scow on a short rope. He is tall, very thin and very hard. Red suspenders hold loose-fitting pants and a battered, sweat-stained hat shades his head. He stands, faded and bent on bowed legs, balancing on stones, leaning a bit against the cold rush of water. He has pulled the scow inch by inch upstream for the last fifty yards. Seven times he has done this before; this time something is different. He is not certain. Perhaps it is diminished strength, his age perhaps, or a random winter change in the river. His face betrays nothing.

He turns his head and stares up the river.
There is no other way.

He raises his arms to pull upwards then lowers his arms to pull down. Nothing. The scow will not go any farther.

He has come over two hundred miles to get here and he has two hundred more miles to go. Now he cannot. For a long time he stands and looks down at the scow. Nothing, absolutely nothing, not a single shade of emotion blinks an eye or bends the seventy-three year old, impregnable face.

He knows that now he is finished. His stiffened hands help him back along the scow. He turns, slips backwards over the shallow gunwale. The current lifts the scow, turns it, and heads it downstream.

The McLeod brothers are
on their own.

Rene Jalbert

The man with the sub-machine guns killed the young woman who greeted him as he came in the front door.

He walked with deadly purpose through the building, blasting the structure and killing anyone who crossed his line of vision. He shot Denis Samson then headed for the Legislative Chamber of the Quebec National Assembly. He killed Camille Lepage on the stairs and stepped into the Blue Room expecting to find the members of the National Assembly; he shot anyone he could see and in frustration at the absence of the Assembly, shot cameras and fixtures, desks and chairs in the beautifully appointed room. There were about ten people in the room. Georges Boyer died from his wounds. Roger Lefrancois died before he hit the floor.

Others were wounded but they hid under tables and behind desks. Rejean Dionne thought he was safe but an errant bullet found his arm. The gunman left the room but returned almost immediately. He threw himself into the Speaker's Chair and furiously sprayed the room with bullets.

Rene Jalbert was the Sergeant-at-Arms for the Quebec Legislature. A former soldier in the famous Quebec Regiment the Van Doos, he saw service in the Second World War and in the Korean War. Nothing prepared him however, for the chaos he saw when he stepped into the building. Bodies, bullets, blood and shards of building were everywhere. The sixty-three-year-old former soldier took off his coat, set down his briefcase and because he was the man responsible for the security of the Legislature,

he walked without hesitation towards the sound of the gunfire. M. Jalbert had been told the assailant was dressed in a soldier's uniform so when he reached the Blue Room he adopted an officer's attitude and shouted with authority. "Stop firing, someone is coming to talk to you." Hearing what he understood as a command, the assailant stopped firing.

M. Jalbert walked in and stood beside the Speaker's Chair. The man in the Chair was very excited, he was pale, his body shook and his face was wet with perspiration. The powerful firearm he held inches from M. Jalbert's chest shivered and jerked.

M. Jalbert was very aware that he might die on this day. It took him almost an hour of careful conversation to talk the young man down. M. Jalbert used the fact that they were both soldiers to build a tenuous bond.

He spoke to the young man with respect and when he saw a flash of blonde hair behind a desk, he suggested they go to his private office where they could speak without other ears or interruptions. This ruse to limit the number of casualties was accepted by the gunman and the two settled in M. Jalbert's office.

With the gunman out of the way, the wounded were attended to. A group of school children were evacuated from a room near the Blue Room. A police S.W.A.T. team filled the halls. It took four hours of conversation before the gunman would discuss surrender. The only police he would surrender to were military police, so Rene Jalbert arranged for him to be placed in military confinement.

A Cross of Valour, to underline his remarkable bravery, joined the other medals on M. Jalbert's chest on a cold Friday in November 1984.

Mrs. Green

Mrs. Green cared for a boy who did not have any sight. She dressed him and fed him and loved him and sent him off to blind school every day. The young man made friends at the school and one day asked Mrs. Green if he could bring a friend to the cottage on the weekend. It was agreed the friend was welcome with his parents' approval.

The day at the cottage dawned bright and calm and the two blind boys asked if they could go fishing. Patient as a rock, Mrs. Green got the rods and hooks and dug a few worms for bait. She took the two boys down to the end of the dock where they sat chatting happily, rods extended off the deep end. The dock was out of sight from the cottage, so Mrs. Green left the door open to hear any yells for help and occasionally walked to where she could see them through the trees. All went well.

On one of her checks, Mrs. Green went down and found the boys still engaged in cheerful conversation. When she got to the end of the dock, she saw for the first time the two boys had their hooks lowered into a boat.

She didn't change them and never told them.

Arthur Nelson?

In 1931, at a cabin on Rat River, Constable Alfred King knocked loudly on the door of a log cabin. He knew there was someone inside but the person would not answer. King backed away and walked the eighty miles to Aklavik because he had gone the limit of the law. In Aklavik, he got a warrant and walked the eighty miles back.

He knocked on the door again. A rifle shot crashed through the door and a bullet smashed entry into King's chest.

The men who had accompanied King, tied him to a sled and raced back to Aklavik. The trip was made in a record twenty hours and saved his life.

A larger force of police and civilians set out in minus forty-degree weather to apprehend the person who had committed such a senseless act. They found the Rat River cabin had been turned into a small fort. Holes in the walls gave the inhabitant protected firing lines and a rifle pit dug in the floor of the cabin protected him from shells fired through windows and doors.

A vicious battle ensued in which no one got the upper hand. The police used dynamite as the light dimmed but the occupant was able to keep them at bay until dark. Cold and lack of supplies drove the posse back to Aklavik. When they returned, the man they had begun to call Albert Johnson was gone. Snow covered his tracks; the posse found nothing.

The posse was sure they could capture the man when they found him camped in a river canyon. Men approached from either side. Bullets flew and the fleeing man fell. The police did not want to walk into a trap so they waited. Again their patience held until the light was low. Corporal Millen rose slowly to approach the fallen man and was shot instantly through the heart. The posse backed off again, this time to a base camp, a few miles away. In the morning they found their prey had scaled the cliff behind his camp and escaped once more.

In Aklavik, Inspector Eames had come to the conclusion that his men had met a fugitive whose wilderness skills they could not match.

No one saw a footprint, a puff of smoke or any sign of the man until tracks were found on the other side of the Richardson Mountains inside

Corporal Millen and three men stayed and searched the Rat River area for a week. Eventually, they found tracks heading off in a wide zig-zag pattern. The zig-zag pattern was ominous because it indicated a man who had enough stamina to walk twice the distance of the men who tracked him and a man who knew how to keep an eye on whoever was following him. Obviously, they were dealing with a man who had run away before. The followers were treated to a range of other evasive techniques. They were following a man who backtracked, left blind trails, hid his tracks in animal trails and who circled around behind them.

the Yukon Territories. Inspector Eames hired an airplane to ferry supplies and to scout from the air. The pilot of the plane, Mr. W.R. May, could see the fugitive from the air. He could also see a group of men on the ice of the Eagle River closing in on him. He flew in circles above the site as bullets cracked back and forth.

On the river ice below, a bullet hit Sergeant Hersey in the left elbow. From his elbow, it spun off to hit him in his knee and then into his chest.

The fugitive was hit. A shot hit his pants pocket where he stored his shells.

The shells exploded, taking off a portion of his hip.
Eventually another shot ended his life.

The search for his identity began. The man
everyone was chasing was originally thought to
be Albert Johnson. Later it was found that a man
named Arthur Nelson, known to have wilderness
skills and a vicious streak, had gone through
the region.

Arthur Nelson killed on impulse. He stole furs
from trap lines and killed trappers when they
complained, leaving a trail of the suddenly
missing behind him.

No one proved the man was either Albert
Johnson or Arthur Nelson. Neither of those men
ever appeared again. Nothing was ever found
that provided the fugitive's identity conclusively.

P.S. In 2007 a body was excavated and
examined for identifying marks and DNA.
To date the results have not been made public.

Wop May & Roy Brown

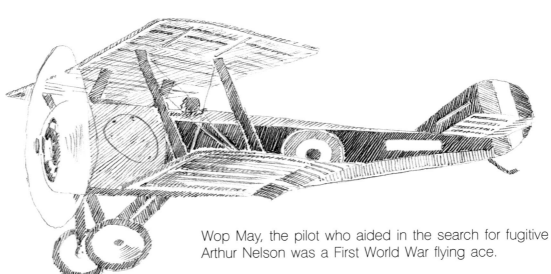

Wop May, the pilot who aided in the search for fugitive
Arthur Nelson was a First World War flying ace.

Mr. May was engaged in his first dogfight over France
when his gun jammed and a red German tri-plane
flipped in behind him and set his sights to kill him.

A Canadian pilot named Roy Brown, pulled in behind the
tri-plane and his shots were accurate enough to force
it away from Mr. May.

As the red aircraft turned to escape Brown, the German
pilot, Baron Von Richthofen, *The Red Baron*, was killed
by a rifle shot from a soldier on the ground.

Mr. Holtz

Mr. Holtz came from Switzerland with his fifteen-year-old wife. They were passing through North Dakota when a new acquaintance told them about better land in Saskatchewan. They packed up and rushed north.

Near Glenbain Saskatchewan, Mr. Holtz found his plot of land. His first duty was to build a shed for their horse with clean new lumber from Swift Current. It took a week to build and the two agreed it was a beautiful shed. Because their money was exhausted, Mr. Holtz put up four short walls of sod and turned the wagon upside down on top to serve as residence for his wife and himself.

Six months went by before the Holtz family was able to improve their comfort level to the standard of their horse.

Joe Boyle

The kid from Woodbridge left a note that read,
"Gone to sea."

Joe had fallen in love with sailing ships on a visit to his brother in New York. He acted immediately and signed on as deckhand on a Nova Scotia barque called the *Wallace*. He was seventeen. When he reappeared three years later, he was no longer a boy or a deckhand. He was first mate and part owner of the ship *Susan*. Captain and crew to a man, described Joe as smart, congenial and a man who would risk his life for his mates.

By the time Joseph Whiteside Boyle was twenty, he had established a pattern he would repeat for the rest of his life. If he loved it, he thought it out, and pursued the success of his interest like a train without brakes.

Joe Boyle fell in love with the quest for gold. Convincing his friend Slavin to join him, the two rushed north and arrived at Skagway before the thousands that were soon to follow. Back then, Skagway was a store, a cabin and a tent. Between the two of them they had half a dollar, so Joe picked up a discarded banjo, tuned it and played for their meals.

Rather than the back breaking climb over Chilkoot Pass, they tried the newly surveyed White Pass. Perhaps the route had been surveyed but no one had managed to mark it well enough to follow. Of the fourteen men who left with Joe and Slavin, six returned to Skagway. Joe went on ahead with the remainder and marked out the first recognizable trail through the White Pass into the Yukon.

The reason for the construction of the White Pass was to help prospectors through to Bennett Lake, headwaters of the Yukon River. The mighty Yukon is a liquid highway that begins in high mountains less than thirty miles from the Pacific Ocean and flows inland. It then makes a five hundred mile sweep past Whitehorse and Dawson, turns northwest and makes a thousand mile loop through the State of Alaska, emptying into the Bering Sea south of Nome.

Dawson and the goldfields were 350 miles down river from Bennett Lake and the only way to get to Dawson was to build, buy or borrow something that could float down the Yukon.

In the Klondike, Joe and Slavin got jobs swinging pick and shovel on Eldorado Claim #13. Just as he had been eager to learn the business of sailing, Joe was eager to learn the business of mining. He worked hard for stake money, adding knowledge and forming opinions as he went. Bit by bit, he bought up claims discarded by discouraged men - his mind full of better ways to work them and other ways to win some of the wealth that surrounded him.

He took note of the fact that many of the people who became well to do, did not become wealthy on a claim. One man sold soup at a dollar a bowl on the main street of Dawson and retired for life after two years of business.

By 1910, Joe owned a sawmill, a narrow-gauge railway and an electrical plant that supplied the city of Dawson with electricity. He bought a huge mechanical mining dredge. A mining dredge is something that looks like an oversized tugboat.

It sits submerged to the gunwales in gravel, while huge buckets take the gravel from the front, put it through a rig that takes the gold out, then dumps the leftovers out the back. The process of digging in front and dumping out the back moves the contraption along slowly and noisily up and down the gravel beds. A good dredge cost $200,000 to build but paid for itself in two months. Never satisfied, Joe brought a much larger dredge into operation in November, 1910. The dredge he named *The Canadian*, had seventy-one huge buckets that scooped the riverbeds for two hundred and twenty-three days of the year and poured gold into Joe's personal funds. He threw away the banjo.

Though Joe had become wealthy, he was not a pretentious man. He cared about his community and the well-being of the people around him.

A church was suggested as a useful embellishment for Dawson. Joe offered to build and pay for the structure. His only requirement was that the new church be non-denominational and available to anyone who wanted to worship in it.

Then the First World War hit the newspapers and Joe remembered how much he loved his country. Joe was going to fight for King and Canada. He leapt into action. Other men his age were given responsibilities but the Canadian Army saw Joe only as an older man with no military training and were not prepared to give him a uniform. Endless appeals and the intervention of impressive people who knew of Joe's abilities, eventually convinced the government to make Joe a soldier.

On September 13 1916, Joseph Whiteside Boyle was gazetted as an honorary colonel of the Canadian Militia and attached to the American Committee of Engineers. The A.C.E. requested he proceed immediately to advise the Russians on the reorganization of their railways.

Russian military railways were in a mess and typically, Joe Boyle had made a thorough study of the mess long before he got to Petrograd.

Unsure of him, the Russians asked him to fix the Murmansk Archangel Line.

Joe stood to speak and took a moment to look each man in the eye. "Do not give me that job," he said, "the Russian Army is about to collapse for lack of supplies. What you need me to do is fix the lines that feed, clothe and supply the brave men who face the Germans. I am prepared to act immediately. I must have a staff of my own men and I must be the only man in charge." Joe's forceful and confidant manner lifted Russian spirits and gave them new hope.

Inside, Joe was not quite as sure as he pretended. He had already learned that any solution would be difficult. He was up against a system tightly knotted by outdated rules and a work force that had been carefully taught their own initiatives always got them into trouble.

For a long time Joe and his staff worked eighteen-hour days without interruption and the railway began to rise from its sickbed. It would have become healthy and robust except that Russia itself had begun to fall apart. It began when the women of Petrograd revolted over the lack of bread. Tsar Nicholas abdicated. German infiltrators seized the opportunity to spread frightening rumours. Foreign agents bought and filled railway cars with useless items so there were no available trains to supply the army. Bolsheviks came out of hiding and violently overthrew their own political system. Russia, already in a death struggle with Germany, became a nation which was either going to die in a war or kill itself in a political struggle. Existence became a puzzle; no one knew who was in charge. Orders given one day were rescinded the next.

The Russians learned to trust Joe's forceful and confident ways and the man in the Canadian uniform with Yukon on the shoulders was next given the duty no one else had been able to solve. He had to untie the *Moscow Knot*.

Not a train could budge. Everything was tied in an unsolvable, unmovable tangle. Moscow had begun to starve. Nothing could get to suffering Petrograd. While Bolshevik bullets whacked and stung in the streets, Joe Boyle and his crew worked on the *Moscow Knot*. He had it untied in forty-eight hours.

Where cars and trains blocked the track, Joe used a bulldozer to tip them into the ditch. If the track was in disrepair, Joe hung up his Yukon jacket, rolled up his sleeves and worked alongside the repair crew.

He amazed Russians who had never seen an officer do physical work before. He earned their trust and affection by swinging a pick or a sledge with the best of them. He stood on railcars like a cheerleader, singing mining songs or clapping his hands to get a rhythm going. When he was stymied by a group of surly men who refused to work, Joe called over a Russian officer who offered persuasive advice to the workers. "Work or I will shoot you." They worked and the job got done.

The outcome of the war began to show itself. The tiny country of Romania decided it was time to declare allegiance to the Allied side.

Joe admired the Romanians' courage and promised to help where he could. He was asked to slip the Romanian Crown jewels out of Russia. German infiltrators spread rumors that Joe was stealing Russian wealth and the race was on. Joe borrowed one of the Tsar's bulletproof railway cars and at full speed smashed his way through Bolshevik roadblocks. A group of the Bolshevik soldiers finally managed to sidetrack the train and warned Joe to stay put or they would blow the train to bits. Joe threw a party, got the soldiers drunk and while they slept he and his men pushed the train down the track with the strength of their backs.

He did not allow anything to stand in his way. When he finally arrived in Romania, he turned over the Crown jewels, fixed the Romanian railway, rescued hostages and at the request of the Romanian government fought to keep the peace between Romania and the new Bolsheviks.

The man who so frequently fell in love with things, found himself loved by the Romanian population. For his accomplishments, he was given the title Savior of Romania and in case that failed to impress him, he was awarded The Grand Cross of the Crown of Romania and The Star of Romania.

The Queen of Romania, was a reigning beauty, intelligent, caring and a relative of half the royal houses of Europe. She touched his shoulder flash and asked, "Vat is dis Yuckon?"

Joseph Whiteside Boyle fell in love once again.

Ada Annie Jordan

Annie had four husbands and eleven children. As she lost each husband, she put an ad in the local newspaper and found a new one.

In 1915, she settled in a secluded spot called Boat Basin where a white sand beach made a fringe for a huge, cobalt blue bay. It was a great place for children when they were well supervised. A submarine popped up one day to take a look and charge its batteries.

Annie built a large garden, ran the post office and the general store. She had chickens and goats and went to great pains to make sure her homestead worked.

Annie prevailed where others could not have done so.

Cougars liked to eat Annie's goats. She shot a lot of cougars to protect her investment, so many in fact, the locals gave her the nickname,

"Cougar Annie."

Paul Kane

He was resting near a fall of water when he awoke to a sense of danger. Through a half-opened eye he saw an aboriginal man crouched and creeping towards him. The aboriginal man did not carry a weapon so Paul lay still. Carefully the visitor reached out and touched Paul's flame-red beard; then with a stunned look on his face, slowly backed away. When Paul sat up, the man ran as though his life depended on it and was not seen again.

Paul Kane was a man with courage and self assurance. He wrote an early Canadian book with the amazing title of -

"Wanderings of an Artist
Among the Indians of North America from
Canada to Vancouver's Island and Oregon,
through the Hudson's Bay's Territory and Back
Again."

In addition to making this trip by foot and by paddle, he completed over five hundred historical sketches. Mr. Kane produced twelve studio paintings. One is missing, five hang in the National Gallery and the remainder hang in the Speaker's Chambers of the House of Commons. The sketches, done in pencil, oil, or watercolour are tucked away in long drawers at the Royal Ontario Museum in Toronto. Paul Kane was born just a few blocks away from where the R.O.M. was later built. His boyhood chums were the children of a Mississauga tribe who lived near his home. When he found there were countless other tribes of aboriginal people in the uncharted west, he wanted to go and draw them.

At the time he left school however, he did not have all of the skills he needed. He put his dream aside for a time and wandered about eastern Canada and the United States drawing local dignitaries, painting signs and anything else that would earn a dollar or two.

He sailed for France in 1841, visited the best galleries in Europe and returned home four years later. On the seventeenth of June 1845, Paul left the town of York on a steamer that sailed to Orillia.

He crossed to Georgian Bay on Lake Huron, and hired an aboriginal guide to get him to Penetanguishene. From Penetanguishene, he got to Owen Sound and from Owen Sound he traveled about forty miles to Saugeen.

Saugeen is where the dead in a war between the Mohawks and the Ojibwa were buried together in irregular mounds.

In a short time he sketched a great many people. He ran into a problem that slowed and diverted him but made it back to York by the last day of November. It was a good trial run. The problem that had diverted him was a man who was so ugly Paul did not want to draw him, so he had to sneak out of town.

Paul went West again in the spring of 1846. He made his way to the Sault and caught a ship for Fort William. The next day he rushed on, by canoe, to catch up with the Hudson's Bay Company's Brigade of Canoes. The Brigade was a group of freight canoes that went on a western circuit to collect the year's catch of fine furs. Sir George Simpson had promised Paul the guidance and protection of the Hudson's Bay Company in his travels farther west. The Brigade canoes were made of birch-bark and cedar; they were twenty-eight feet long and about four to five feet across. Each carried eight men and twenty-five packs. On the way west, the packs contained supplies. On the way back, the supplies were replaced by bundles of furs. The packs were in ninety-five pound units because that was the amount men could carry over rough ground.

The next spring, again with Paul Kane in tow, the Brigade traveled west to Dog Lake and Dog River, through many lakes and many portages to Lake of a Thousand Islands. Then across Sturgeon Lake and up the Maligne River. The Maligne River area contained aboriginal people called "Weedigo" or "people who eat human flesh." From three o'clock in the morning until one hour before dark each day, the Brigade paddled without pause until it reached Fort Garry.

After arriving at Fort Garry Manitoba, Paul went across the western prairies to Jasper, Alberta, crossed the Rocky Mountains and went down the Columbia River to the Pacific Ocean.

After a brief stay to draw a people known as Flatheads, he turned around and came back.

In his book, his experiences are described with painstaking care. Chapter headings read like penny thrillers: Blanket of the Dead, He Devil, Young Assassin, Thunder Point, the Silver Bullet, Camping among the Slain, Lost Man and Little Rat to name a very few of very many.

Travelling back was different than travelling out. A trip down the Columbia took fifteen days but to paddle against the current on the way back, took over four months.

During the trip, Paul was accused by an aboriginal community of causing the death (by stealing her likeness) of a woman he had previously drawn.

Another adventure was being introduced to a woman so beautiful her path was covered with otter skins by her admirers.

The book with the exceptionally long title and with its long list of adventures also contains a list of the drawings and paintings Paul rendered on his trip to and from the west.

A sketch of Paul Kane's painting "The Death of Big Snake." c. 1856.

Works by Paul Kane can be seen in venues other than The Royal Ontario Museum in Toronto. They are also in The National Gallery in Ottawa, Montreal Museum of Fine Arts, Glenbow Alberta Institute and the Stark Foundation in Texas.

Harry

Wigwam Harry lived in Whitehorse. His home was a discarded
piano crate. He made a modest living with his skills as a
sleight-of-hand artist and as a dancer. When no one needed
those skills, Harry was a pick and shovel man. Harry dug a
basement for a man in three days. When the fellow decided
not to pay him, Harry returned to the site and filled it back in.

Archie Baloney

His real name was Archibald Belaney
but everyone called him Archie Baloney.

He was an Indian he said and he had a frog in his pocket. The other kids could be the cowboys but he had to be the Indian. For a kid in the seaside town of Hastings, England, this was unusual but then the young man whose name was Archie Belaney had always been different.

His father had gone off to live in North America; Archie lived with two maiden aunts and he always had something ghastly in his pocket. He practiced throwing knives into trees and built beaver dams in the creek. Archie read all the works of James Fenimore Cooper, then all of Ernest Thompson Seaton's adventures. He was a dreamer and loved to write.

At eighteen, Archie took a ship to Halifax and a train to Toronto and as soon as he could, he went north to Cobalt. At nearby Lake Temiskaming, an aboriginal family took a liking to him and promised to teach him the ways of the North American Indian. Archie was a willing worker. He tramped through the woods on snowshoes and his enthusiasm for life in the woods helped him to become very good at it. In the summer, the family moved from their trapping grounds to a spot further south on Big Bear Island where there was a band of one hundred Ojibway. Archie became friends with a young woman named Angel Egwuna and the Egwuna family invited him to spend the following winter with them on their trap line. Archie was in heaven. He was living his dream, learning how to survive in the woods and learning the life skills of the aboriginal people. He didn't seem to mind the disadvantages of this kind of life. He gloried in it, soaking it up like a thirsty man. He was so attentive and interested, the Ojibwa people named him Ko-hom-see or "Little Owl."

He became an expert trapper and woodsman. After a time as an adopted member of the aboriginal families, Archie began to feel and look like an Aboriginal. He gorged on all they had to teach him and these generous people accepted him as one of their own. He had learned from the Ojibway to respect his environment, learning to take only what he needed.

Sitting in the conferences of the Ojibway, he listened to their problems and watched the democratic process that produced their solutions.

He felt a growing respect for their opinions and their ways.

In 1893, one of the problems that was an irritation not only to the aboriginal but also for the white trappers of the region, was the closing of a prime trapping area, known today as Algonquin Park. Shortly after the Park area had been taken away from the trappers, it was learned the park officials had decided to earn some money on the side by trapping the region themselves, illegally.

The situation became a game. Stories of the attempts to get around the park rangers enlivened many a meeting or conversation. Trapping was not only profitable, now it was fun. The Rangers patrolled the perimeter of the Park. One trapper waited for the beginning of each snowstorm to have his tracks filled with new snow. Another walked with his snowshoes on backwards to give the appearance of a man exiting the Park rather than entering it. One agile trapper disguised his tracks by walking for miles on stilts.

Archie was very proud of the prowess he had in the bush, and in a conversation with several trappers, he claimed he was a good enough woodsman to enter the park at the southwest corner and exit at the northeast boundary without being caught. More tracks for the rangers to chase meant more trappers could enter the park successfully. The game was on.

Just to prove there were rangers who were good woodsmen too, ranger Bud Callahan caught him before he had gone a half dozen miles. They had to camp for the night and before Bud woke in the morning, Archie was up and gone. Now the game became a race. Bud followed Archie to where he had fallen through the ice in a beaver pond. Bud saw where he had struggled and from the tracks in the snow, knew Archie was in trouble as his body responded to the cold. Both feet were thoroughly frozen. Bud caught up and helped him to continue until they reached the ranger's cabin on Canoe Lake. Over a period of three weeks, ranger Mark Robinson nursed Archie back to health. Archie and Mark became fast friends and when Archie was better, Mark gave him some clothing and money to get him back to Temagami.

A little ashamed of himself, Archie moved to the Mississagi River area and did his best to become a better woodsman and a better person. He worked as a fire ranger for the Ontario Forestry Department and having had some success writing articles for his old school magazine, he settled down, put his mental shoulder into it and wrote two books, *Men of the Last Frontier* and *Tales of an Empty Cabin.*

In 1915, Archie enlisted in the Canadian Armed Services and went to do his duty in the First World War. The Germans very kindly shot off two of his toes in the battle of Ypres. Archie's toes didn't work too well anyway after their freezing experience so the complete absence of two didn't make a big difference. He returned to the bush to work as a trapper and a ranger.

In 1920, an Ojibway family again took him in. Alex and Anny Espaniel promised to teach him aboriginal skills that would help him to live off the land.

He experimented with pretending to be an Indian and went as far as inventing an Apache mother and a Scots father, a story he would often rearrange to suit his needs.

By 1926, a lot of first time trappers were trying to make a living in the woods. Archie was disgusted with their cruel methods. They were in it for quick money only. An aboriginal always left a mating pair of beavers in the pond to produce a future crop of pelts. The first-timers didn't care, they killed them all. A trapper's rule of thumb stated that any month with an "R" in it guaranteed a good pelt. The new trappers did not know that even though April had an 'R' in it, the baby kittens were too young. If you killed their mother they died. None of this activity honoured what Archie saw as the intelligent environmental concepts of the aboriginal. Archie was disgusted. He became a conservationist and an advocate for aboriginal rights.

In 1928, he declared himself the president of The Society of Beaver People and began to write. An article for Country Life was so successful, he was asked to write a book.

As 1929 arrived, more and more people became interested in the preservation of the wilderness. Archie began to travel to speaking engagements. He appeared in aboriginal dress and continued to tell the story of his aboriginal beginnings. If he wanted to "come clean" and tell everyone he was really Archie Belaney, it was too late. As his role of conservationist expanded, he began to call himself Grey Owl.

As Grey Owl, he extended his work into films and articles for the Parks Department, the Canadian Forestry Association and the Boy Scouts. Archie became famous. People travelled from other countries to hear him speak. He travelled to England twice, where crowds of one thousand and more cheered him on. He was asked to give a command performance at Buckingham Palace and he visited his two aunts in Hastings where he had tea in full Aboriginal regalia.

Through these years, there were people who knew the famous Grey Owl was really Archie Belaney. Most of them respected the conservation job he had taken on. A few, perhaps with a little jealousy for his fame, called him Archie Baloney.

Archie Belaney was forty-five years ahead of his time in the field of conservation.

Agnes Macdonald

No one had asked to do that before
and because she was the wife of John A.,
they decided to let her try.

John A. and Agnes rode in comfort along the shores of Lake Superior, past Lake of the Woods and into the flat prairie. They saw Buffalo and grass fires and a wall of storms that lined the horizon. Wind played in the trees and a storm fought to a dramatic end. This was only the second time in Canadian history a vehicle that rode on rails was able to cross the country. John A. said he was too busy to go but Agnes persisted and he decided to make the time. He was the Prime Minister after all and responsible for the railroad's construction.

On the west side of Alberta, where the Rocky Mountains rose to startle passers-by, the train paused in the town of Banff. A proud engineer took time to explain the power and beauty of his mountain engine to his passengers. Agnes saw the flat area above the steel teeth of the cow catcher and recognized it as the best seat in town. She was going to sit there all the way to the Pacific Ocean, she said. There was a flutter of disagreement but she got her way and a butter box was placed on the cowcatcher with a blanket for the cold of the mountain heights.

The train with Agnes as outrider pushed down the valley and gained speed for the climb to the continental divide. She pulled the blanket around her body. Downhill was fun until the engine reached a speed she deemed unnecessary and headed seemingly, straight for the side of a mountain. Agnes tied down her hat, got off her butter box and found something to hang onto. At the last moment, a hole appeared and the world went black.

A light came on above her. How did they know there wasn't something they would run into in this cave? A tiny pinhole of light showed ahead and they exploded into the sunshine.

Two startled men, standing by the track, managed to raise a hand to the woman riding the cowcatcher. The cowcatcher caught a wild pig and threw it violently past the outrider but by now the train had had its fun and slowed to a more sedentary pace. The Kicking Horse River flowed past, then the mighty Columbia.

She wasn't tired or bored for a second. Her breath left her as they raced over a trestle, high above a mountain stream. As if to compete for her approval, another tressle crossed in clouds. There was nothing below and nothing very far ahead. In the valley, grass glowed golden in lowered light, the sky turned grey-green then purple. A pastel valley inched past to reveal a deep green lake that became in turn the mighty and black, Fraser River. With dramatic intention, the mountains inched aside to show the many fingered delta of the Fraser.

From time to time, someone came to the cow-catcher to keep an eye on Agnes. They need not have worried. Agnes was unharmed and filled with the joy of seeing all the sights that until now she had only been able to imagine.

Sioux Lookout

On fur trading expeditions, the Sioux always
sent their best warriors backed by a
contingent of women trained to fight.

Lookouts for a small Ojibwa band camped
on Lake Superior spotted the Sioux approaching.
The band packed up and fled along the water highway to Pelican Lake.
They hid their women and children on a small island and on a high place, made a camp they
knew the Sioux would attack. Archers were positioned on the hill above the camp. Two groups
of the strongest men were hidden on opposite sides and around the corner of the hill. The elderly
men of the camp collected their fishing lines and stood on the shore looking busy.

The Sioux spotted what appeared to be an unprotected camp, ran past the old men and attacked.
As they arrived at the camp site, they were quickly diminished in number by the arrows from
above. The warriors, hidden around the corner arrived in time to kill those who wanted to run
away. The old men put down their fishing gear and eliminated the threat of the women in the
canoes.

The lookout that spotted the approaching Sioux was standing on a high point where today's
community of Sioux Lookout now stands.

Konwatsi-tsiaienni

Konwatsi-tsiaienni was a beautiful young woman who had been schooled in the English mission school and at eighteen travelled with her Mohawk elders as an advisor in their transactions with the governments of the time.

William Johnson was the Superintendent for Indian Affairs in the British colonial province of New York. He was a wealthy and successful trader and a politician who admired the Mohawk custom of having their women play a leadership roll in finances, selection of chiefs, and if and when to fight. William Johnson recognized Konwatsi-tsiaienni's abilities and hired her to manage his large home. His home normally held ten to thirty guests who expected three meals a day. Eight to ten of the guests were Mohawk sub-chiefs. An English visitor to the house described Konwatsi-tsiaienne as having beautiful features and a calm dignity. In time, the manager of the house became the common law wife of William Johnson. Together, they produced eight children.

About the time thirteen American colonies decided they didn't want to be British any longer, William Johnson died prematurely at fifty-six years of age.

The mother of his children moved to a place nearby and opened her own trading business. Her neighbours had become tired of trying to say her name and now called her "Molly". Her loyalties were British and through her trading establishment, she transferred military information to the British military and assisted the Loyalist side in whatever manner she could.

Molly was credited with boosting the morale of the Loyalist side and soon found it necessary to run north to avoid an American jail.

She and her eight children escaped through Fort Niagara and a large portion of the Mohawk community followed close behind.

When the war ended, the Crown showed its gratitude to Molly and the Mohawk people by giving Molly a substantial military pension and a stone house at Cataraqui. The Mohawk people were given a tract of land along the Bay of Quinte.

The Elder Son

???

173.

The authour packed his bags and left for a film shoot. The plan, to meet his client in Calgary was successful. The client was a frightening intellectual from New York, a published poet, philosopher and a difficult convesationalist. His choice of subject on the drive to Drumheller was 'courage'. Eventually, the authour calmed the intricate exchange by telling him this story:

A man hitched two teams of work horses to a heavy chain with a shackle on the end and attempted to pull out a stump that had been in his way for many years. The chain broke and snapped back like an elastic band and struck the man in the head with great force.

He died instantly.

The man had fathered two sons, both gone to fight in World War II and were not there to bury him. Mother was left alone on a New Brunswick farm.

On June 4th 1944, two days before "D" day, the boys got the terrible news and after a long discussion, decided they had to finish the job they were involved in at the moment. As soon as they could, they would return home to work the farm for their mother.

Two days later the boys were in separate but adjacent parts of the Third Canadian Division as it landed on Juno Beach. The landing plan was flawed. Anti-personnel mines had not been removed from the beach because flail tanks had not arrived and underwater barriers slowed the arrival of landing craft.

Enemy firepower was well positioned and extreme. When the doors of each landing craft splashed down and the men charged ahead, they were faced by dead and dying soldiers that covered the beach from ocean to sea wall. Enemy fire sliced into them before they got down the ramp.

With amazing courage, the living jumped over the dead, raced down the ramp and up the beach. The elder brother charged up the beach, jumped one body, sidestepped another and began again to run. He stopped suddenly, turned and ran back. The ripped and twisted remains of the body he had just sidestepped were what little was left of his brother.

Slowly, without regard for explosions, air full of bullets and his corporal's screams, the older brother walked to a burned-out armoured vehicle and climbed inside. His mind was filled with thoughts of his mother and how she could be left completely alone. He stayed in the vehicle until the fighting stopped.

When the authour had completed the story, he turned to his client and asked, "Was the older brother courageous?"

Silence ensued for the remainder of the trip.

Halifax 1917

Lieutenant Garnet Colwell went looking for Gwen Westhaven. They had gone to the theatre the night before. He never found her.

Vincent Coleman saw the burning ships approaching the dock outside his building. He was informed that one of the ships was loaded with explosives and he started to run. His steps faltered, he stopped, turned and ran back to his desk. Once there, he grasped the key of his telegraph machine and sent a message to the fast approaching passenger train to tell them of the danger. The train stopped. Vince Coleman died.

Doctors didn't sleep. One took twenty-two pieces of glass from Archie Upham's head. Another worked to keep Annie Liggins alive. She was buried in rubble for twenty-six hours. A doctor put eyes in a bucket; too many people had been looking out the windows when the explosion erased the town. A doctor put a bandaged baby into the arms of a grateful mother. It turned out the baby was not hers. Her child was never found.

The two boys still looked a little rough, so Mrs. Driscoll gave them a dollar for two haircuts and sent them to the barber in Truro. The barber put on the neck cloth, then the sheet, aimed the scissors and put his hand on the boy's head. The boy squealed in pain and yanked away. The barber apologized and took a closer look. The child had shards of glass and splinters of wood embedded in his head. "Ahh," said the barber, "you're from Halifax." The barber called in a friend who could also cut hair and the two of them set to work on the two boys, washing and cleaning and eventually cutting their hair. The older of the two boys, the holder of the dollar, was concerned about the price the barber would charge for all the work expended.

When it came time to pay, he held out his dollar but the barber said, "Put that away and both of you come with me." He took them across the street and bought them both a full set of new clothes.

The little girl could move; it was simply her choice not to. She had been in the living room of her house when she was lifted into the air, clothes torn away, then swished and whirled two blocks away where she was thumped down onto the grass. The grass was beside a walk that once served a house that was no longer there. Beside the walk was an overturned wagon and a dead horse.
The sailor hurried by, obviously on a mission to somewhere. He stopped, then retraced his steps to look down at the girl. He took off his pea jacket with the brass buttons, carefully covered the little girl and rushed on.

To honour the generosity of the people of Boston Mass., who sent thousands of tons of aid to the devastated city of Halifax, Nova Scotia sends the city a giant tree every Christmas.

Marguerite de La Rocque de Roberval

Jean-Francois de La Rocque de Roberval
was given the appointment of
Lieutenant General of Canada
by King Francois I of France in 1540.

Jean-Francois was given the privilege of establishing a new fortified town at Charlesbourg-Royal on Cap-Rouge. He was given the privilege and three ships but not the money. It was assumed Jean-Francois would be able to carry it off because he came from a very important French family.

It is difficult to blame him for his tone of self-importance because he was the son of Bernard de La Rocque, the Governor of the French City of Carcassone de Languedoc-Rousillon and a Gentleman of the King's Household. If that wasn't enough, his father was an officer of the Comte d'Armagnac. If asked, he would also be able to say his grandmother was Alix de Popincourt, Lady de Roberval in Picardy. It will come as no surprise then, that when Jean-Francois de La Rocque's sixteen-year-old niece Marguerite took a liking to a handsome male commoner, he and the family saw their status threatened and took great offence.

Marguerite de La Roque, who had been used to getting her way, said she loved the commoner and no one could stop her from marrying him. A family conference decided that the embarrassment could only be avoided if Jean-Francois took Marguerite to the New World.

King Francois I had given Jean-Francois de La Rocgue the *Valentine*, the *Anne* and the *Lechefraye*. The three ships were to depart immediately with adequate supplies to start a new colony.

A deep-sea captain named Jacques Cartier was secured as guide and left in May 1541. Jean-Francois departed with beautiful Marguerite aboard. The family's problem appeared to be solved. Shortly before arriving in St. John's Newfoundland, two things changed everyone's opinion. The handsome young commoner was discovered below decks and Marguerite de La Rocque de Roberval was found to be with child.

Events can be turned to good or evil depending on a person's intelligence and disposition. Marguerite's actions appeared to be a blatant affront to her uncle's authority both as a captain and as leader of the King's expedition.

His status was challenged and he was furious.

After collecting fresh water and supplies, the expedition was on its way. We don't know exactly which route Jean-Francois took to the interior; we do know he made a detour. Jean-Francois de LaRocque stopped at two small islands, named Iles des Demons and put Marguerite, her manservant and her young lover ashore. They were given one ancient musket with powder and shot and just enough food to starve to death slowly. Jean-Francois sailed away with his reputation as a less than generous human firmly reinforced.

The baby died shortly after birth. The young man, who probably had great expectations for a life of ease, lost his mind and died shortly after the baby. The manservant lived for seventeen months, then he too died leaving Marguerite alone. Marguerite buried them all in a spot where the rocks weren't too close to the surface.

She knew how to load and fire the musket and this kept her alive for more than a year. A shot from the musket eventually alerted a Breton fishing ship that returned her to France and her family. In the meantime, Jean-Francois's temperament had helped to cause the failure of his mission to establish a new colony.

The Colony collapsed after one winter. He returned to France where both he and the project were identified as failures. France did not attempt to open another New World colony for fifty years.

On the other hand, Marguerite returned to extensive applause for her survival. Her story caught the interest of the French populace and the King's Geographer, Andre Thevet. M. Thevet was so inspired, he wrote an account of the interesting drama. Fifty years later, M. Thevet's successor, Samuel de Champlain, read Andre Thevet's story of Marguerite's survival and was convinced to act on Marguerite's determination and courage.

The two small Iles des Demons that were at the northern tip of Newfoundland disappeared in the mid-17th century.

On the morning of April 14 1915, Fredrick Hall rushed for the second time into an open battlefield at Ypres to rescue a wounded man. On his first try, two volunteers who went with him, died.

At the Somme in the fall of 1916, Leo Clarke was alone when he attacked twenty enemy soldiers. He was wounded but continued to fight furiously until the enemy ran away.

In 1917, Robert Shankland fought heroically in a battle at Passchendaele. In the battle, Mr. Shankland survived, 16,000 Canadian soldiers did not.

When these three men were given the Victoria Cross for their bravery, it was discovered they all lived on Pine Street in Winnipeg, Manitoba.

The Pine Street sign was taken down and replaced by a sign that now reads Valour Road.

Mr. Rutherford was sent to fight in France, where early in his career his actions earned him a Military Medal and a battlefield commission. On August 16 1918, he won the Victoria Cross for capturing forty-five German soldiers. At Monchy-le-Preux in the middle of frantic fighting, he found himself alone with only a side-arm and facing a troop of enemy soldiers. He shrugged, stepped forward and demanded their surrender. To his amazement, they all raised their arms.

Later he found an orphaned Lewis gun and captured another thirty-five prisoners.

He didn't fight in the next World War. He taught young officers at the Royal Military College in Kingston, Ontario.

The bridge was covered with dead and dying Canadian soldiers. There was overwhelming gunfire from the opposite river bank. Charles Merritt knew the bridge had to be taken so he led his men up one side and was wounded as he went down the other. He was wounded again as they worked to clear a group of enemy positions.

When he was ordered to withdraw, he refused to go himself and stayed to cover the departure of his men.

He was the only prisoner taken.

All eyes were focused forward into the night where there was always a danger of running into something, when suddenly the forty-five foot fishing troller *Respond* began to rise skyward. Tiki the dog crouched, the two men grabbed handholds as the rise continued and the ship began to tip. Continuing to roll and from high in the air, the ship made a crashing descent, upside down into the water. Tiki and the two men, scrambling for their lives, found themselves in a small pocket of air trapped at the top of the overturned hull.

The *Rimba Meranti* was a huge lumber carrier with a bulbous nose. It had come up behind the tiny fishing boat and lifted it onto its nose.

The noise the troller made as it tumbled into the sea was heard by the crew of the larger ship and they immediately notified the Canadian Coast Guard.

Two R.C.M.P. divers arrived in record time due to a hovercraft that could do eighty kilometres an hour and Constable Robert Teather slipped over the gunwale into the dark waters. Underwater access to the ship was blocked by a tangle of lines and it took time for him to tie them out of the way. Inside the steerage cabin, there was no light and a confusing mix of oil, gasoline and snowfall of dog kibble. Teather felt his way and eventually found a trap door in the former floor that led to the engine room and the bottom of the boat. He found the two men and the dog in the air bubble at the top.

Both men were in bad shape, aware the bubble was decreasing in size.

Robert motioned for the first man to hang on behind him and showed him how to use the air hose. They descended towards the cabin door but when the opening proved to be too narrow for two men, the fisherman panicked. He ripped the breathing apparatus off Robert and locked himself around his neck. Fighting the man on his back and his own panic, Robert wormed them through the opening and got to the surface where he could load the fisherman onto the rescue craft. Arrangement had been made for the two officers to take turns but Robert realized it would take too long for the second officer to find his way. Bob had been badly frightened by the close call and did not want to go back but knew there was no other way.

He turned and descended again into the black. The second man, the fishing boat's captain, was calmer and fit through the hatch better than the first.

The boat was towed to shore and as soon as they arrived, another diver rescued Tiki. She was excited by her adventure and very much alive..

Robert Teather

The torture techniques of the Sioux were very effective. Freemantle lasted until she knew another round of torture would kill her. She gave up and agreed to show the Sioux warriors where her village was. Her legs didn't work any more so they carried her to her canoe, gave her a paddle and propped her in a position so she could use it.

Sioux warriors travelled a long way from their tribal lands to hunt and prove their courage. Torturing a woman was not very courageous but it was one of their ways of searching out places to plunder. In the villages they did find, they raped and killed at random. Freemantle's refusal to tell them where she lived was her attempt to protect her people.

Feebly, Freemantle picked up her paddle and eased her canoe into the current. The current pushed her downstream. What the Sioux did not know, as they piled into their canoes, was Freemantle's village was upstream. The fit and amply muscled warriors followed her for a long time, just a few canoe lengths behind.

Freemantle

They were startled when the woman they thought was almost dead suddenly sat erect, grasped her paddle in a firm grip and put on speed. To gain the advantage of a faster current, the Sioux moved their canoes into the middle of the river. Freemantle was much closer to the shore where she didn't have to fight rough water. Even with the better current, the Sioux had a hard time keeping their freight canoes even with Freemantle's smaller and lighter canoe.

The river took a sharp corner. Freemantle cornered even closer to the shore and once she was around the bend, grabbed an overhanging branch and pulled herself to a stop. Half way around the corner, still in the middle of the river, the Sioux saw mighty Kakabeka Falls a short distance ahead and did their best to get out of the fast current.

It was too late, Freemantle had timed it perfectly. The Sioux all died in the foam and boulder bottom of Kakabeka Falls.

Kathleen Evans

Her time, her truck and her project.

At eight o'clock in the morning, the old van pulls onto the road and works up to speed. Behind the wheel, hands at ten and two, seventy-five year old Kathleen Evans sits on a cushion to get a good view of the road. This is her truck, her choice and her retirement project.

The van is second hand; not hard to tell. A friend has covered the inside walls with wooden shelves and on the shelves are four hundred children's books secured tightly in place. The books are the best Kathleen can find. Her route is sixty-four farms long. At the end of the route, she will turn around and do the route again to cover the kids she missed. If a child shows a particular interest, Kathleen goes to Edmonton and finds books to feed that interest. Even boys are interested.

Kathleen was a teacher for forty-one years. As soon as she retired, she built her project and her route to give children who didn't live in town, the benefit of well-written words and ideas. She has seen the children grow and blossom. She will do this for as long as she can.

The van door shivers open and rattles shut. Cows comment. She waves goodbye, eight more families to visit today.

Robert Service

There are strange things done in the midnight sun
By the men who moil for gold;

Robert wrote his first poem when he was six. His maiden aunts taught him to be frugal. On their way to church, they encouraged him to take longer strides so that when his feet hit the ground fewer times, it lengthened the life of his shoes.

Mr. Service emigrated to Canada from Scotland and lived for a time on Vancouver Island. He travelled in British Columbia and the Western United States. After a time in the Yukon, he visited New York, then the Southern States and Cuba. He returned to the Yukon by walking and paddling two thousand miles via the Athabaska River, Great Slave Lake, Fort Simpson and Fort McPherson. He carried his canoe over the Great Divide and came back down into Dawson via the Bell and Porcupine Rivers.

In 1912, he worked as a war correspondent in the Balkans for the Toronto Star and journeyed to Vienna and Budapest. He moved to France and married Germaine Bourgoin. When the army turned him down as a soldier, he returned to the job of war correspondent. At the same time he also wrote reports for the Canadian Expeditionary Force and served the American Ambulance Service as a driver.

After the war, he spent time in Paris and Brittany. In 1938, he travelled to Moscow and then down the Volga River and across the Caucasus Mountains to the Black Sea hoping to find a way home through Poland. Hitler had just invaded Poland so he snuck

out through Estonia and Sweden, then made his way home. He brought his family out of Brittany and moved to Hollywood where he was given a small part in a movie with John Wayne and Marlene Dietrich. The story they were filming was one Robert Service had written.

During his travels and the few times he settled in one place, Robert Service wrote eighteen books of verse, six novels and two extensive auto-biographies. Mr. Service is well known in Canada and known best for two poems he wrote in the Yukon, *Dangerous Dan McGrew* and *The Cremation of Sam McGee*.

There have been people who criticised Robert's casual style and street level focus. His answer for their complaint, "I only write poetry for people who wouldn't be caught dead reading poetry."

Another answer to criticism was his poem:

*"Love smote the Dreamer's lips, and silver clear
He sang the song so sweet, so tender true,
That all the market place was thrilled to hear,
And listened rapt – till came the Man Who Knew,
Saying:"His Technique's wrong: he singeth ill,
Waste not your time! The Singer's voice was still.
And then the people roused as if from sleep,
Crying; "What care we if it be not Art!
Has he not charmed us, made us laugh and weep?
Come, let us crown him where he sits apart!"*

Throughout his life Mr. Service loved to walk.

After a day's work at Dawson's Bank of Commerce, he would have something to eat, don his winter gear and his snowshoes and walk in the moonlight for mile upon mile, his head busy with poetry or prose. He was a solitary man seen by the people around him as kind and genteel. He did not participate in the wild ways of people who loved a rougher life; he watched and was observer and reporter of people we might otherwise know little about.

It was from Robert Service that we gained not just knowledge but feelings for his style of poetry.

Poems such as:
"The lady that's known as Lou"
"Sam McGee from Plumtree"
"Salvation Jim who knew mining from "Genesis to Revelation"
"Pine boughs freighted with lace and gems and a stillness that made silence seem like sound."

He said vice was more interesting than virtue, and so he wrote and wrote and rhymed and wrote.

He was seldom seen in public without his banking suit and his four inch stiffened collar. The collar underlined a calm and handsome face that did not show emotion. He wrote a poem about the red-coated police but didn't mention famous Sergeant Sam Steele who lived down the street. Neither did he write about Joseph Boyle who built the church and supplied the town with electrical power.

He cared less for the rich or famous and loved the ones who struggled. It was his feeling that the well-to-do didn't need him. Salvation Jim, the lady named Lou and the boys at the Malamute Saloon did.

Robert Service loved to tell stories with a turn or twist that would amuse his reader.

"I hailed me a woman from the street,
Shameless, but, oh, so fair!
I bade her sit in the artist's seat,
and I painted her sitting there.
So I painted a halo round her hair,
And I sold her and took my fee,
And she hangs in the Church of Saint Hilaire,
Where you, and all may see."

Robert Service's cabin.

Mount Rae

Mount Rae has a porcupine side that sits next to the continental divide. From her northern slope, the Elbow and the Sheep gather their first trickles. The Elbow joins the Little Elbow and they dance along together past the ashes of Kanouses's Post and the death lodge of a whiskey trader. They arrive together at a place called Clear Running Water.

At Clear Running Water, the waters of the Elbow join the muscled Bow, offspring of the Wapta ice fields. Together they amble across the prairie, past Arrowood and Crowfoot, then corner around Jumping Buffalo Hill, down past Hays and the Badland Hills. Near Purple Springs, the Bow and the Oldman marry, to have and to hold.

The two rivers that are one turn northward, now known as the South Saskatchewan. They soothe the clays of Redcliffe, then slip past the spot they call the Medicine Hat. At Empress, the South Saskatchewan grabs the Red and they make a run for it across the width of Saskatchewan. Laughing and leaping, the South Saskatchewan and the North Saskatchewan tumble together and run eastwards, now calmly, now proud and no longer diminished by their directional designations.

This is the mighty Saskatchewan. The Saskatchewan kisses sweet Carrot River and pours the sum of its contributions into the arms of Lake Winnipeg. Lake Winnipeg blushes with pleasure and holds its wealth until it is time for it to be given to the Nelson.

The Nelson River with care and appreciation for the labours of the many contributors, carefully tips the trickles of Mount Rae into the arms of Hudson's ocean-like Bay.

Mina Hubbard

A petite person whose strengths
were intelligence and determination.

As information came in, Mina began to believe that the attempts to rescue her husband were carried out without appropriate enthusiasm. When she found that Wallace was going to return to Labrador for another attempt to explore from North West River to Ungava Bay, she was enraged. Mina began immediately to plan a trip of her own that would put her in direct competition with Wallace. It would be natural to think of a woman who is going to walk seven hundred kilometres in rough under explored country as a woman of substantial dimensions. In reality, Mina was a petite person whose strengths were intelligence and determination.

As her travelling guides and companions, Mina chose four men with extensive experience in wilderness travel. George Elson was the son of a Scots/Cree carpenter, woodsman and cook. George's friend Joseph Iserhoff was from the same Hudson Bay post and was the son of a ship-wrecked Russian sailor who married an aboriginal woman. The third male member of the crew was Job Chapies, a man "raised in a canoe" who handled the craft with unusual skill.

Chapies was the helmsman in Mina's canoe throughout the trip. She tells of wanting to ride facing backwards in the rapids just to watch his concentration and skill.

Mina Hubbard hated Dillon Wallace.

In 1903, Dillon Wallace and Mina's husband Leonidas Hubbard had embarked on an expedition to map the parts of Labrador covered, but not detailed, by early surveyor A.P. Low. Mistakes were made in supplying the Wallace & Hubbard expedition and after finding they were unable to gather enough food, they turned around. Mr. Hubbard became ill and was left behind while the others went for help.

Winter arrived and Leonidas Hubbard died before they could rescue him.

Dillon Wallace wrote an account of the ill-fated attempt . Mina thought the account diminished her beloved husband and put far too much emphasis on Mr. Wallace's abilities.

The last member was young Gilbert Blake, a Labradorian of mixed Scots and Inuit descent. Gilbert had an endlessly positive attitude and had worked as a trapper since he was twelve. He was easy going and loved to laugh. His father trapped deep within Labrador and was one of the men to bring out the body of Leonidas Hubbard in the winter of 1904.

Mina started out from North West River on June 27, 1905. Dillon Wallace left soon after. Mina had her four skilled and proven experts. Wallace's crew consisted of a geology student from Columbia University, a student from a school of forestry, a handyman and an Ojibway from Minnesota. These five were accompanied for a short time by Duncan McLean, a trapper from North West River. Shortly after McLean left them, they encountered troubles caused by their ignorance of effective routes.

Mina had taken the time to learn map making and how to get an accurate idea of her whereabouts using a sextant. Throughout her travels from North West River, up the Naskaupi River, across the height of land at Lake Michikamau and down the George to Ungava Bay, she took the readings that would make her trip useful to those who followed.

If Mina Hubbard had any uncertainties about her safety travelling in an unknown land with four tough, wilderness men, she never showed it. The men found Mina thoughtful and caring and they supported her in return. Further into the trip, they began to bring her little gifts of tiny pink flowers, a ptarmigan wing, a stone and the blue flowers that grew in moss on high hills and showing her things they knew about and loved themselves. The men teased Mina as older brothers might and she took it in the right spirit. The good natured teasing and Gilbert's infectious laugh became two important factors that cemented the team into a happy, cohesive, mosquito-bitten group.

The trip was not an easy feat to accomplish. Each day consisted of lifting, climbing, and carrying packs for long distances. Mosquitoes, flies and an island covered in spiders took turns trying to drive them insane. Mina devised a protective head cover that would have been great for Halloween but the men warned her Indians would shoot her if they saw her wearing something like that. Days contained as many as eight portages, when the canoes had to be emptied, their contents transported with many trips over rough ground. Then the canoes them-selves had to be carried to the new place of departure.

When the group got to caribou country, they stood in amazement as thousands of caribou passed by close enough to touch. A large male crossing the river, pulled them for a distance as Gilbert held his tail. When the animal reached the other side of the river and began to climb the bank, he kept pausing and looking back at them as if to ask, "What was that all about?"

Then Mina got lost.

The men were aware that she liked to step off the trail to investigate and she could not always keep up with their rapid pace. They explained that these little absences worried them and would she please be careful. A particular hill promised Mina a good vista for her camera and she asked the men if they would allow her to climb it. It appeared not to have too many dangerous places so they armed her and watched her go. She climbed the hill and disappeared over the top. When the appropriate time for her to reappear came and went, they stepped calmly into the woods and began to search. As time passed and they became more and more concerned, panic set in, their pace quickened and they began to run here and there, up over the hill and around the bottom looking in holes and in the water. They shouted her name and fired their guns. They grew certain they had lost her.

To a man they began to cry. When she finally struggled out of the bush bruised and bitten, they were so upset none of them would speak to her.

Instead of the bull strength of paddling and poling that it took to reach the height of land, the team now needed a new set of skills to navigate explosive downhill rapids and the sudden vertical drops of the George River. The rapids alternated with areas that were as dark and smooth as a quiet lake but tipped downwards in the direction of the fast flowing water.

Mina had arranged for the coastal supply ship *Pelican* on its regular visit to Fort Sveright, to pick them up at the bottom of the George River. Now, they began to worry they might not have travelled fast enough to make their *Pelican* connection. If they were late they would have to stay until spring or return to North West River by dog sled in the dead of winter.

They attacked the George enthusiastically and enjoyed the thrilling race downhill. Instead of three or four km. a day, the last days above the Hudson Bay post of Fort Siveright produced runs of twenty-five to thirty-five km. per day.

Mina and her team of expert woodsmen completed their trip within the time allotted and without hunger, wounds or grudges, fifty days ahead of Wallace.

Mina Benson Hubbard was the first woman to cross Labrador.

Not long after she met Harold Ellis.

David Thompson

David walked, paddled, rode horseback and
dog-sled over 80,000 miles in the early West.

Mr. Thompson was a decent man who had a singular ability to irritate everyone. The source of the irritation was his burning enthusiasm for everything he bumped into.

At seventeen, he spent a winter in the tepee of an old Cree named Saukamappee. There he learned to value the culture and preferences of the First Nations people.

At eighteen, David was forced to recuperate from a broken leg in the home of Philip Turnor, the Hudson's Bay Co.'s principal surveyor. Mr. Turnor watched the young man ignite as he learned mathematics and astronomy. From that day forward, David carried a sextant and always knew exactly where he was.

The Hudson's Bay Company didn't value mapmakers as much as the North West Fur Company, so David switched horses and was hired by the North West Fur Company as their astronomer and surveyor.

He was sent off to explore the upper Missouri Valley and to find the headwaters of the Mississippi. The job was expected to take two years but David was back in ten months, full of energy and a smile on his face. A cluster of angry men dragged along behind him.

Mr. Thompson, almost single handedly, found and noted every nook and cranny of the soon-to-be Canadian West. He covered 80,000 miles on foot, horseback, canoe and dog-sled and then compiled seventy-seven volumes of journals about its biology, ethnology and geography.

Mr. Thompson was sent to claim the watershed of the Columbia River but John Jacob Astor beat him to it by coming up the west coast in a ship and claiming the bottom quarter. Instead, David Thompson discovered, explored and was the first white man to travel the full length of the Columbia River. Other explorers in search of a route to the Pacific had ignored the Columbia River because when they crossed the Rockies, they saw a river that flowed north. David found the northward flowing Columbia did a huge loop around the Selkirk Mountains and headed south into Oregon. This route became the fur traders' most economical route and was used until Canada got its railroad.

Besides wearing out everyone he worked with, David did something else. He refused to sell liquor to the First Nations people. He treated every man with equal respect. When he married a First Nations woman, he asked her to accompany him on his travels. Unlike other traders who rejected their "country wives" and brown skinned children, David brought his wife Charlotte and their children to Montreal where the children could access good schools and learn the language and customs of other people.

G. O. Sutherland

He liked the people
and he liked the place
so he bought a blanket and stayed.

Eventually G.O. Sutherland got a job on a tugboat that plied up and down the lake. Because he put his mind to it, he very quickly worked his way up to captain. The tug towed logs for a lumber company at Robson.

Robson was conveniently placed at the bottom of the lower Arrow Lake. Groups of men with lumber permits cut logs along the lake and it was Mr. Sutherland's job to run the tug up the lake to collect them. Mr. Sutherland continued to like where he lived; he met a beautiful woman, married her and together they produced a fine family.

The Arrow Lakes are a broadened portion of the Columbia River. The Columbia starts in the southeast corner of British Columbia and runs north, turns around, then heads back south in a five hundred mile loop. The loop collects snowmelt and rainwater from the Purcell and the Selkirk Mountains, two mountain ranges caught in the five hundred mile loop. When the Columbia gets down to Robson at the bottom of the southern Arrow Lake, it drops the disguise of a lake and turns back into the mighty and muscled Columbia.

The river crosses the U.S. border and continues southwest for another six hundred miles until it empties into the Pacific Ocean.

Mr. Sutherland's tug worked the portion of the river north from Robson for the full length of the lakes and then entered the northern river portion and travelled up for a hundred or so miles until he could access the Columbia Reach. "G.O." turned around in the Reach and headed back home adding logs to his boom as he went. This trip produced plenty of logs but as time went on, because of the generous nature of Captain Sutherland, his tug became the Arrow Lakes water bus and delivery service. He would stop to pick up isolated families and run them up or down the lake according to their needs.

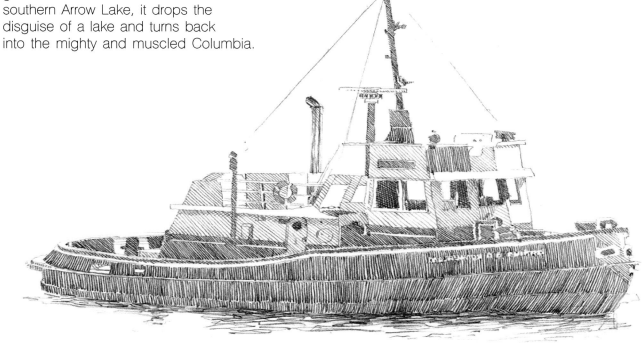

A new tug on the lake has been named the G.O. Sutherland to honour the driver of the Arrow Lakes bus.

The King

He won a contest for best thank-you letter to the fire department. When summer came, he and twenty other children flew out the doors and windows of the two room schoolhouse. Their summers were joyful and filled with the things they liked to do. No small town could stifle their imagination. They whittled willow whistles, played baseball and made crystal sets. They boxed, wrestled, held yo-yo contests and did their chores. They played a game with knives thrown into a circle drawn on the ground and traded steelies and glass marbles. They reduced the gopher population and played on the walls of the river that flowed past the town.

At a place in the wall of the Red Deer River, the letter writer built a throne, two stones for arms and a flat stone for a seat. He sat in comfort in his high place and dreamed.

J. D. Dempster

The valley when I finally get there seems empty. A strong haze from a large forest fire in Siberia has travelled its thousands of miles to shade detail in the farthest mountain wall. There are no sounds, maybe a timid whimper of wind. I thought it would be colder.

In Whitehorse, I had rented a little red zipper for a car. Now I get out and sit in the grass well off the road. The young woman who rented me the car, wanted to take it back when I mentioned I was going "up the Dempster." "It'll get all scratched, there's icky oil trucks with rigs that throw gravel." I promise to watch for trucks throwing stones and when I reach the valley, at mile sixty-two, I pull well off the road to accommodate her concern. The Blackstone River ambled through the middle of the valley, sometimes running narrow, sometimes spreading in a silver wash, wall to wall. A lot of the valley was covered in thick brush. The First Nations must have come through here in the winter. The river ice would be easier to travel on rather than fighting scrub and swampy places.

During the Ice Age, western glaciers stopped their travel eastward within sight of this valley. Eastern glaciers travelling west stopped on the eastern edge of this same valley.

First Nations people, exploring across the Bering Land Bridge, had found this corridor and used it to go south into the central portions of North America. We would not have had a population of First Nations people in North America if this valley, like all the others, had been plugged with glacial ice. Through the haze to the west, I can just see the Tombstone Mountains with their sharp, canine teeth. Beyond this place, I travel through an area of mountains so ancient and crushed by cold and ice, nothing sharp remains. I have never seen soft round mountains before.

Before I am finished with the valley, I sit for a time where the Blackstone River runs up on the permafrost. It was at this spot, the Lost Patrol passed by on their way north. When they attempted to return

south and became lost, Corporal Dempster came rushing past this place in minus fifty-degree weather. He was rushing with good intentions; rushing too late.

The patrols to the north coast of the continent were instituted by the Canadian government to make it clear to American whalers that tiny Herschel Island was Canadian. Herschel Island lay in the Arctic Ocean just off the north coast, in the Beaufort Sea. It became a problem when it began to be used as a way station for American whalers, who flew the American flag.

Whaling was a lucrative business at the turn of the century. Each Bowhead whale had seven hundred and eighty bones in its mouth. The bones were harvested and used as stays in corsets. In a corset-crazy time, each whale produced $10,000 worth of stays as well as oil and meat.

To help to identify the land as Canadian, the Government asked the Royal North West Mounted Police to run up to Hershel every now and then to wave the Canadian flag. A route was chosen that began at Dawson City and ran north along the Blackstone, Wind and Peel rivers to Fort McPherson, along the coast and across the ice to Herschel Island.

The trip, made on foot, was four hundred and seventy-five miles each way. The patrols were always carried out in the dead of winter by dog sled. Great caution was taken with a full understanding of the need for exceptional strength and fortitude to overcome the perils of bitterly cold winter travel.

The patrols began in 1904 and ended when things seemed secure in 1921. Only one trip ended in tragedy. It was led by an experienced constable named Frank Fitzgerald. We don't know what was in his mind but this man with proven strength and experience made mistakes that remain hard to understand.

On the seventh patrol, this time from Fort McPherson south, Frank Fitzgerald neglected or was unable to supply his patrol with enough of the correct kind of food to last the length of the trip.

Also, for the first time in the history of the patrols, he did not engage a guide from the Loucheaux group of Aboriginal people. The Loucheaux were the best cold weather woodsmen in the world and even they found the exceptionally long trek to be on the edge of their abilities. This mistake alone could have cost the lives of the four men who froze to death on the banks of the Peel River. Fitzgerald and his men never got this far south to the spot where I sit in the grass. When they finally admitted to themselves they were lost, they turned around and tried to make it back. They got to within thirty-five miles of Fort McPherson but lost the strength to continue. They tied a handkerchief to a branch on the river bank to mark the place where they would die.

I wonder what Dempster thought when he first saw the handkerchief fluttering alone in the brush on the bank of the river.

It was a wonder more men were not lost over the years. The trip was made without a weather forecast and in temperatures that dropped to eighty degrees below zero. No one worked out wind chill factors in those days. Uncovered skin froze in thirty seconds. A cup of hot coffee poured towards the ground, was frozen before it got there.

The traditional point where the R.N.W.M.P. trail crosses today's Dempster Highway is at mile sixty-two. Corporal Dempster passed nearby, two weeks too late.

I have seen it. I climb back into the zipper and wheel it around. An oil truck brakes to see if I'm in trouble. That's something everyone does on the only road in North America that goes above the Arctic Circle.

Billy Stanger

A kid from Winnipeg named William Samuel Clouston Stanger, got a field promotion to sergeant in the First World War before he was nineteen. This was probably the least remarkable thing he did in his long lifetime. As an infantryman, he was gassed and sent back to England to recuperate. There, he learned to fly and became a member of the Air Force. Back in Europe, he shot down the Red Baron's brother and eleven other German pilots. His technique was to fly so low he could stampede the German horses that were pulling wagons of supplies and shoot officers' cars off the road. By the end of the war, he was a Captain in the Air Force with decorations that included the Distinguished Flying Cross and the Military Cross.

Along the way, his name was changed to William Samuel Stephenson. After the war, Mr. Stephenson became a wealthy English industrialist and often travelled to Germany to buy steel. On one of his trips, he became aware that Hitler was cheating on Germany's First World War promise not to build an army. Everywhere Stephenson went, he saw that Hitler was hiding military expenditures to build a new army, navy and air force. This clear violation of the Treaty of Versailles implied a growing Nazi threat to those who were willing to see it. British Prime Minister Neville Chamberlain and others didn't want to know; opposition M.P. Winston Churchill did.

Mr. Churchill and Mr. Stephenson became fast friends, Stephenson supplied Churchill with specific information and photographs of the intelligence he had collected. This information put Churchill in the position of knowing more than his Prime Minister about the things Hitler was up to.

When World War II was underway and Churchill was Prime Minister, he needed someone he could count on to run the British Security Co-ordination unit in New York City. Stephenson was given the job. The job immediately expanded to include all the British Intelligence agencies, MI5, MI6, SOE (Special Operations) and PWE (Political Warfare Executive).

Bill Stephenson's real job was to ease the American people towards participation in the war. One of the first projects he embarked upon was to build an essential information bridge between the secret organizations of the United States and Great Britain.

As the war developed, Churchill used Stephenson as his contact with the American president Franklin Roosevelt. Stephenson had access to all the secret intelligence from Europe. He passed on the parts he saw as important to the relevant American organizations. To reassure himself that everything would be secret, Stephenson hired Canadian women and R.C.M.P. officers to staff his offices in Rockefeller Center, New York.

He wisely hired a University of Toronto electrical engineering professor from Moose Jaw, Saskatchewan, named Benjamin deForest Bayly. "Pat" Bayly created *Rockex*, a fast (one minute instead of three hour) and secure system that was adopted by all of the Allies for secret communications. When a training facility for wartime operations became necessary, Bill Stephenson's BSC organization set up Camp X near Oshawa, Ontario. Two thousand British, American and Canadian covert operators from ISO, OSS, FBI, RCMP, U.S. Navy and U.S. Military Intelligence and future members of the CIA were taught how to kill silently, blow things up and run secret communications systems.

Ian Fleming, who wrote the James Bond series, trained at Camp X.

Camp "X"

Bill Stephenson, the *Quiet Canadian*, became Sir William Stephenson in 1945. In 1946, he was the first non-U.S. citizen to receive the American Presidential Medal for Merit.

BIBLIOGRAPHY

2. Joseph Barss – Bandits and Privateers. H. Horwood & Butts, Doubleday. ISBN 0-88780- 157-9 /privateerdays.com
5. Lablonsky, Stephen – Raincoast Chronicles Harbour Pub.
6. Harry Morren – Frontier Book #21m F.W. Anderson.
9. Alan Fleming – Word of mouth.
11. Myra Bennett - Newfoundland Newspaper and magazines.
16. Matthew – a family story
17. Grant McConachie – Bush Pilot with a Briefcase – Douglas- Macintyre. ISBN 1-55054-586-8 / Alberta Online Encyclo-pedia Canadian Pacific Airlines / Family info.
23. Lillian Ailing, Beautiful British Columbia Magazine.
26. Mr. English – Shipwrecks Vol. 2 -M.McCarthy Creative Publishers / ISBN 0-921191-15-4/ Gov. of Newfoundland. Railway Coastal Museum
30. Charles Taylor - A family story
33. Rod Stamler - Above the Law, Paul Palango, ISBN 0-1710- 6929-4 / McClelland & Stewart
38. A Tall Man & a Short Man. – Word of mouth stories.
41. Dorothy – Buried Treasure Elnora History Com. – Valley of the Dinosaurs –Friesen Publishing – ISBN 0-88925-836-8
45. Fredrick Creed. – Discovery Channel
46. Jeremiah Jones – The Black Battalion – Calvin Ruck Colchester Historical Society ISBN 0-9690119
47. Emma Edmonds – The Beaver Magazine, August- 2002
48. Sam Steele – Robert Stewart – Centax Book Pub. – ISBN 1- 894022-23-8 Forty Years in Canada – S. Garrod / Archives.
56. George Edwards – Bill Miner – Frank Anderson ISBN 0-919214-18-5 /Outlaws – F.W. LindsayThe Daring Escapes of Bill Miner / Stan Sauerwein Interred With Their Bones – Peter Grauer
59. The Boy in White Shorts – W. Irish
60. Robert Salts – Never Alone,Robert Salts.ISBN0-9681567-0-3
64. Robert Hampton Gray – A Formidable Hero – Stewart Soward –Stewart & Sowart Pub. – ISBN 0-9690703-9-X / CFB Esquimalt Museum
61. Jerry Potts – The Riders of the Plains – A.L. Haydon – Hurtig / Jerry Potts Plainsman – Glenbow Museum – ISBN 0-919224-87-3 Dictionary of Canadian Biography
69. Tom Three Persons – Glenbow Museum / Mary's Genealogy Treasures of the Lethbridge Herald.

71. A. McNaughton – Vimy – Pierre Berton McClelland & Stewart –ISBN 0-7710-1339-6 Canadian Encyclopedia Historica / High Beam Research
73. John Brown – Waterton Guide – http://www.peakfinder.com
76.. Ethel Catherwood – Time Magazine – April 29, 1996
77. Stony Chief – W. Irish
78. Wilfred Grenfell – Grenfell of Labrador – Ronald Romprey –ISBN 0- 8020-5919-8 / Remarkable Past - Pierre Berton – ISBN 0-7710-1357-4 / Wikipedia / Can. Encyclopedia Historica
82. The Boy – Word of mouth
83. Deerfoot – Dictionary of Canadian Biography Online. http://www.biographi.ca Glenbow Museum
84. Alexander Mackenzie – Roy Daniels – Oxford University Press – ISBN 0-19-5140186-7 First Across The Continent
86. Three Sisters. - Word of mouth
87. Three More Sisters - The antique car rep.
88. Peter Pond – Glenbow Museum
89. James Morris – Sable Island Shipwrecks – Lyal Campbell ISBN 1- 55109-096-1
92. Crowfoot – Hugh Dempsey – Goodread – ISBN 0-88780-155-2 / J.MacGregor, Hurtig / Wikipedia / Glenbow Museum/ Riders of the Plains - A.L. Haydon – ISBN 0-88830-38-7
96. Laura Ingersoll – Fitzhenry & Whiteside – ISBN 0-88902-202-X / Legendary Canadian Women – Carol McLeod – ISBN 0-88999-215-0 / Niagara Heritage Trail / Wikipedia / Winnipeg Museum
99. Jean McWilliam – Glenbow Museum – March April 1972
100. George Dixon - The Haligonians Roma Senn ISBN - 0-88780-671-6 Wikipedia / International Hall of Fame.
102. Nellie McClung – The Beaver – October, 1993 / Legendary
104. Tsawwassa – Fur & Gold – John Pearson
106. Dobbin – St. John's Uni. & Newfoundland papers.
109. Mathew Simser – C.B.C. Report
110. Angus Walters- The Saga of the Bluenose – Ernest Robinson Vanwell Publishing Ltd. ISBN 1-55125-009-8
112. Mrs. Copeland – Sable Island Shipwrecks , Lyal Campbell ISBN 1-55109- 096-1
113. Louise Arbour – wikipedia – Canadian People –http://en.wikipedia.org
114. Arthur – a family story.
117. Ghost Devil – Nancy (Angel) McLeod
118. Otis Hyslar. – A family story
119. Jung Mah – a family story from Jung Mah
120. Robert Rundle – Glenbow Museum, Calgary
122. Lumber Jacks – Family story
124. Miiki & Morita Obasan – Joy Kogawa – ISBN 0-14-006777- 9

127. Lefty – W. Irish
130. Mervin, Albert – a family story
133. Illingworth Kerr – a family story
134. Daniel McGinnis –Oak Island – Millie Evans –
     ISBN 0- 920427-39-1 /BBC Home Page –
     Mystery of Oak Island / Money Pit
     Mystery / Oak Island Treasure Company
140. Romeo Dallaire –Shake Hands With the Devil,
     R. Dallaire, ISBN 0-679-31171-8
141. Bob Bartlett – Harold Horwood/ Doubleday –
     ISBN 0-385-25245-5 Brigus Museum / The
     Log of Bob Bartlett – Blue Ribbon Books /
     Bondoin, Arctic Museum.
144. Albert Failles – National Film Board of Canada
     Nahanni
147. Rene Jalbert – Cross of Valour –Melady –
     ISBN 0-590-71510-0
149. Mrs. Green – A family story
150. Arthur Nelson – Pirates & Outlaws of Can. –
     Horwood & Butts Doubleday – ISBN0-385-
     18373-9
152. W.R. May – Pirates & Outlaws
153. Mr. Holtz – A family story from Shawn Doyle
154. Joe Boyle – The Sourdough and the Queen,
     Leonard Taylor- Metuen Publishing – ISBN 0-
     458-96810-2 schools/projects/
     canadianhistory/josephboyle.html
159. Jordan, Ada Annie – Cougar Annie's Garden -
     Horsfield. Salal Books ISBN 0-96077008-1-4
160. Paul Kane – Wanderings of an Artist – Paul
     Kane – Hurtig – ISBN 0-88830-084-0
163. Harry – Up There Magazine, 2005
164. Archie Baloney – Grey Owl – Jane Billinghurst
     Greystone –ISBN 1-55054-692-9 168. Agnes
     Macdonald – Fur & Gold / The Bio Lady
     Macdonald – Louise Reynolds / Van Hornes
     Road, ISBN#0-919130-22-4
171. Konwatsi-tsiaienni & Joseph Brant -
     Wikepedia
172. The Elder Son – Word of mouth.
174. Halifax, The Barber, The Doctor, The Sailor,
     The Telegrapher –Shattered City, Janet Kitz.
     Wimbus. ISBN# 0-921054-11-4
176. Marguerite de La Rocque de Roberval – Just
     a Minute – Boulton –ISBN 0-316-10369-1 /
     ancestries.com / Wikipedia
179. R.C. Rutherford – Marching to Armageddon –
     Mort & Gran– Lester Gorpen Dennys
     Publishers - ISBN 0-88619-209-9
179. Charles Merritt – True Canadian Heroes on the
     Battlefield –Arthur Bishop – ISBN 1-55-267-
     868-7– Winnipeg Central Library
180. Robert Teather – Cross of Valour – ISBN 0-
     590-71510-0
181. Freemantle – Ontario Parks Dept. sign at
     Kakabeka Falls
182. Kathleen Evans. – Canadian Broadcasting
     Corporation.
184. Robert Service – On the Trail of –GW
     Lockhart – Luath Press Ltd., Edinburgh.
187. Mount Rae – W. Irish

188. Mina Hubbard - The Woman Who Mapped
     Labrador. Buchanan, Hart& Greene –
     McGill, Queen's University Press.- ISBN 0-
     7735-2924-1
192. David Thompson – McGillvray, Lord of the
     Northwest – Clarke Erwin & Co.Ltd. / The
     Beaver – June, July 2002 /David Thompson –
     Barbara Belyea
194. G.O. Sutherland – Information provided by
     Mr. Sutherland's family and the Revelstoke
     Museum.
196. The King – a family story
198. J.D. Dempster – The Lost Patrol – Dick North
     Raincoast Pub
200. Billy Stanger – Encyclopedia of Canada.

56 colour illustrations.

*The illustrations were painted over a period of seventeen years.
They are all glazed oil on masonite and are usually 5 feet x 4 feet for the landscapes
and 30 inches X 40 inches for the two paintings with flowers and berries.
All of the original images have been committed to other owners but
for anyone who would find one useful, the images can be purchased in print form.*

CPSIA information can be obtained
at www.ICGtesting.com
Printed in the USA
LVIC05n0915091214
417843LV00001B/1